# NUKAZUKE

## The Japanese Art of Fermented Pickling

Nami Yamada

**TUTTLE** Publishing

Tokyo | Rutland, Vermont | Singapore

# Contents

**Assorted Pickles, pages 26–34**

**Futomaki Sushi, page 93**

**Chapter 3**

# A Nukazuke Pickling Calendar and a Troubleshooting Guide

**Chapter 4**

# Recipes Using Nukazuke Pickles and Nuka Pickling Mash

**Chilled Horse Mackerel and Rice Soup, page 94**

**Stir-Fried Summer Vegetables and Pork with Miso, page 101**

**Chapter 5**
# The Health Benefits of Nukazuke Pickles

# An Invitation to Nukazuke Pickling

Nukazuke is a traditional Japanese method of pickling in a bed of fermented rice bran and germ. Generations of home cooks in Japan have kept a barrel or crock of this richly aromatic mash tucked away in their kitchen as an easy way to incorporate delicious, healthy fermented food into their daily meals. Establishing the bed is simple, and once active, it can pickle a nearly endless range of ingredients in hours or days.

The detailed instructions and recipes in this book will help you make nukazuke pickling part of your own life. Before you know it, mixing the bed and adding foods to pickle will become a simple daily ritual. You can take out the fermented foods when you feel like eating them and mix the pickling bed quickly while you're at it. Skipping a day here or there doesn't matter.

Nukazuke pickles are rich in plant-associated lactic acid bacteria, and their many health benefits are attracting renewed interest in Japan. Microorganisms are said to resonate with the human heart. I hope you will nurture your pickling bed with the same care you would give to a child or a pet. The microorganisms will surely respond to your care by giving you delicious nukazuke pickles.

–Nami Yamada

# What is Fermentation?

Many fermented foods are familiar mealtime staples, as you will see in the list of common fermented foods starting on page 122. Some of them may surprise you. Nukazuke in particular is rich in plant-associated lactic acid bacteria (lactobacilli), which improve gut health, and thiamin, which relieves fatigue, boosts appetite and promotes digestion.

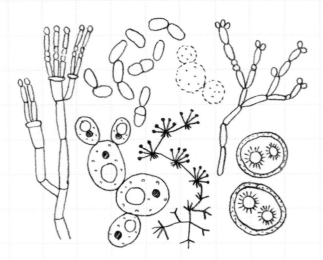

### Microorganisms
"Microorganism" is a generic term for bacteria such as lactobacilli; fungi including molds, mushrooms and yeasts; and other organisms too small for the human eye to see (approximately .04 in [1 mm] or less). They are found everywhere in nature, including inside the bodies of humans, animals, and other living organisms.

What changes take place in the pickling bed to transform ingredients into tasty and nutritious nukazuke? Let's start with the general mechanism of fermentation.

### The basics of fermentation
Fermentation occurs when microorganisms (see note above) attach themselves to foods such as vegetables, meat, fish or milk and metabolize them as a source of nutrients, producing a variety of flavor compounds and nutrients that were not present in the raw materials.

The enzymes in microorganisms catalyze the breakdown of proteins and starches in the foods. This creates nutrients such as amino acids, sugars and vitamins.

If the end result of microbial action is beneficial to humans, we call it "fermentation," and if the end result is undesirable, we call it "rot." In other words, fermentation and rot are the same thing from a microorganism's point of view. The difference depends on the type of microorganism involved and how we humans perceive the outcome. For example, natto

Written with the assistance of Shigeo Miyao, Doctor of Agriculture (Professor, Tokyo Kasei University; Visiting Professor, Sichuan University; Vice President, Japan Traditional Foods Research Association; Senior Advisor, Japan Federation of Pickle Cooperatives)

Microorganisms attach to a food and start metabolism (energy conversion) using the components of the food as a nutrient source. Enzymes in the microorganisms break down proteins and starches to produce amino acids, sugars and other substances.

The Fermentation Process

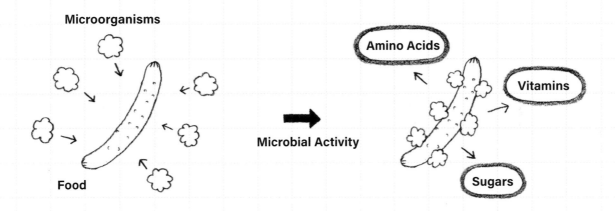

(fermented soybeans) is a delicious fermented food for many Japanese, but may be seen as rotten and smelly by people in other countries. On the other hand, Swedish surströmming, a canned salted herring that is famous as the world's stinkiest food, is a fermented product that Japanese people have a hard time enjoying.

**Microorganisms involved in fermentation**
Of the various microorganisms involved in fermentation, koji mold (*Aspergillus oryzae*) is most familiar to Japanese people. In fact, it's often called the "national fungus" of Japan. Koji mold plays an active role in the production of sake, miso, soy sauce, and other beloved foods. Acetic acid bacteria, another type of microorganism, convert alcohol into vinegar. The microorganism that produces alcohol is a type of yeast.

Lactobacilli, yet another type of micro-organism, are indispensable for making nukazuke and yogurt. There are various types of lactobacilli, more than one of which live in the nukazuke pickling bed.

# How Nukazuke Fermentation Works

**The fermentation process in a pickling bed**

Let's take a look at how the microorganisms in a nukazuke pickling bed produce flavor components and nutrients beneficial to our bodies. The nukazuke pickling bed consists mainly of rice bran and germ (together called nuka) and salt (see page 16). When vegetables and other foods are buried in the bed, they release water due to osmosis caused by the salty bed. At the same time, their nutrients dissolve into the bed. Proteins and carbohydrates from both the vegetables and the nuka are broken down by the metabolic activities of lactobacilli, the microorganisms in the bed, to produce flavor components such as amino acids and lactic acid, which are sources of umami.

As the vegetables lose water, these flavor components enter them. The vegetables also absorb nutrients and vitamins from the nuka. The end result is highly nutritious nukazuke pickles.

**Lactobacilli in the pickling bed**

The lactobacilli in the pickling bed are naturally occurring bacteria attached to the nuka or vegetables. There are many other microorganisms in the bed as well, but lactobacilli can live in an environment with little oxygen, and since they are salt tolerant, they grow easily in the salty medium. For these reasons, lactobacilli quickly multiply in a nukazuke pickling bed.

Yeast can also survive in the salty, acidic environment produced by lactobacilli, and an ideal pickling bed has a good balance of lactobacilli and yeast. However, mold is also resistant to salt and acid, and can begin to grow if the bed is not mixed enough. This is why daily care of the bed is important.

**What makes nukazuke delicious?**

Several factors contribute to the delicious flavor of nukazuke pickles, including the umami from amino acids, the refreshing sourness and aroma of the lactic acid produced by lactobacilli, and the rich flavor from the yeast. This complexity explains why you can eat nukazuke pickles every day without getting tired of them. The moderate saltiness also makes it a perfect side dish for plain rice. A certain amount of salt prevents the growth of bacteria that cause food poisoning and other harmful microorganisms, improving the keeping quality of nukazukc.

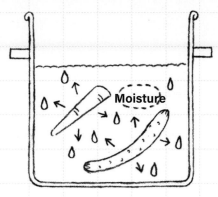

Nutrients from vegetables in the pickling bed seep into the bed along with moisture in the vegetables.

**Lactobacilli**

Lactobacilli feed on nutrients from the vegetables. They produce amino acids, lactic acid and other flavor components that are the source of umami.

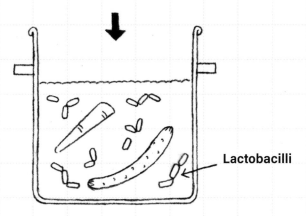

To learn about the health benefits of the abundant nutrients absorbed by nukazuke pickles, see p. 118.

- Thiamin
- Lactic Acid
- Flavor Components

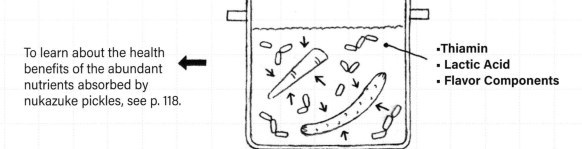

Amino acids, lactic acid, and thiamin, which bran naturally contains, soak into the vegetables, creating delicious nukazuke pickles.

**Chapter 1**

# The Nukazuke Pickling Bed

Nukazuke starter kits containing a ready-made bed can be purchased online, but making your own from scratch and slowly developing it to suit your taste is much more rewarding. All you need are a few ingredients and a little time. In this section, you'll find detailed information about the ingredients, equipment and process of making your own pickling bed.

# How Nukazuke Pickles Are Made

Making a pickling bed is simple, but it can't be rushed. The timeline below gives a rough idea of how the bed is made and when you can start eating the pickles.

**Day 1**        **Day 2 on**

### Make the pickling bed

First, gather your storage container and ingredients. Mix the ingredients thoroughly and pack into the container.

### Mix the bed daily and make "throw-away pickles"

Mix the mash by hand every day and bury scrap vegetables like radish leaves and the outer leaves of cabbage in it. Discard the scrap vegetable after several days and repeat. Continue this process for 10 days to 2 weeks to mature the bed.

**10 days to 2 weeks later**

Throughout this book, the fermented mixture of nuka, salt and water shown here is referred to as the **pickling bed** when it is in the pickling container and the **pickling mash** when it is removed from the container.

### The bed is ready. Time to start pickling!

When you smell a sour aroma coming from the pickling bed, you'll know it has fermented enough. Now it's time to start pickling vegetables to eat. Depending on the season and type of ingredients you use, pickles can take from 4 hours to 1 week to ferment.

# Pickling Containers

Several types of container work well for storing your pickling bed. Be sure to choose one you like because you will be using it every day for a long time.

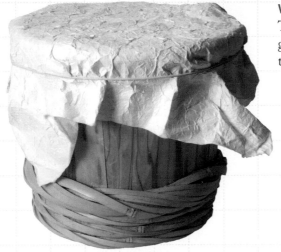

### Wooden Barrel
The advantage of wooden barrels is that they have good airflow and absorb moisture. The downside is they are prone to dryness, insect infestation and odors.

### Ceramic Jar with Lid
Ceramic jars are ideal for pickles because they resist acid and salt and keep odors contained. They also maintain a relatively stable temperature regardless of the room temperature.

### Enamel Containers
Enamel containers are acid- and salt-resistant, stylish, and keep odors in. A rectangular container can fit nicely in the refrigerator.

### Lidded Plastic Containers
Plastic food containers can be used if you want to pickle a small amount, pickle fish and meat separately, or keep the pickling bed in the refrigerator.

### Small Ziplock Plastic Bags
Convenient for pickling fish, meat, soft tofu and similar foods separately from the main pickling bed. They also store easily in the refrigerator.

## Nuka, the Heart of the Pickling Bed

*Nuka* refers to the bran and germ of rice, while *zuke* means "pickles," so nukazuke translates literally as "bran and germ pickles." As the name suggests, nuka is the most important part of the pickling bed. A byproduct of polishing brown rice to produce white rice (see illustration to the right), nuka contains about 95% of the nutrients in rice. For nukazuke pickles, use fresh, raw, pesticide-free nuka if possible. Because nuka is high in fat and oxidizes easily, turning rancid, avoid raw nuka that is not fresh. Fresh raw nuka has a sweet flavor similar to toasted soybean powder (*kinako*). In Japan, the best place to find it is a rice processing facility.

Outside of Japan, it can be purchased on the internet, but may not be fresh. To be sure that the product contains both the bran and germ of the rice, search for products labeled as nuka or *kome nuka*, or marketed specifically to make nukazuke. If raw nuka is not available, it is fine to substitute toasted nuka (*irinuka*). It is not as flavorful as raw nuka, but is less prone to insect infestation and has a longer shelf life. If you are not using raw nuka immediately, you can freeze it or toast it. To toast it, heat in a skillet over medium-low for 2 to 3 minutes, stirring constantly, until it smells nutty and fragrant, being careful not to burn it.

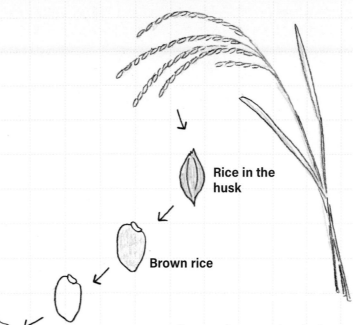

**Rice in the husk**

**Brown rice**

**Germ rice**

**White rice**

Grains of rice are threshed to remove the husk, producing brown rice. Partially polishing the brown rice to remove the bran produces germ rice. Polishing it more to remove the germ produces white rice. The Japanese term "nuka" refers to both the bran and germ that are removed in the milling process.

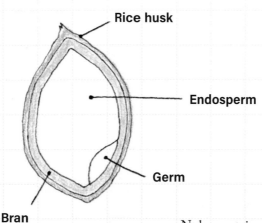

**Rice husk**

**Endosperm**

**Germ**

**Bran**

Nuka contains the bran and germ that is removed when brown rice is polished. Although these parts make up only about 10% of the rice kernel, they contain 95% of the nutrients, including protein, fat, and B vitamins. White rice is the endosperm that remains after polishing.

# Basic Pickling Bed Ingredients

Because the pickling bed is so simple, it's important to be particular about the ingredients.

**Raw nuka**

Use freshly milled, pesticide-free raw nuka. If raw nuka is not available, toasted nuka may be used (see p. 14).

**Salt**

Use a ratio of 10% to 12% salt to nuka. Natural sea salt is recommended.

**Water**

Adjust the amount of water according to the dryness of the nuka and the room humidity. If using tap water, let sit overnight or boil for 15 minutes to remove chlorine. Cool to about 104°F (40°C) before using.

**Mature Pickling Mash**

If available, adding mash from an established pickling bed will speed up the bed's initial maturation process.

**Dried kombu and red chili peppers**

Kombu adds umami and chilies have antiseptic properties and slow the oxidation of fats. They are always added to the pickling bed.

# Ingredients to Add Flavor to the Pickling Bed

Add optional ingredients as desired to create a unique pickling bed.

### Roasted soybean powder (*kinako*)

Rich in glutamic acid, an umami component. Add about 1 tablespoon per 2 pounds (1 kg) of pickling bed.

### Bonito flakes (*katsuobushi*)

Rich in inosinic acid, an umami component. Add about 1 tablespoon of finely shredded flakes per 2 pounds (1 kg) of pickling bed.

### Dried shiitake mushrooms

A treasure trove of the umami component guanylic acid. Add about 1 mushroom per 2 pounds (1 kg) of pickling bed.

### Yuzu

Add in winter when this fragrant citrus fruit is available. Zest and blanch the peel briefly, chop finely, and add about 1 tablespoon per 2 pounds (1kg) of pickling bed. Try other citrus too.

### Garlic

Has antibacterial and antiseptic properties. Too much makes the entire pickling bed smell bad, so only add one clove per 2 pounds (1kg) of pickling bed.

### Sansho pepper

Sansho has antiseptic properties and adds a fresh aroma. Blanch fresh whole pods in hot water for 10 minutes, drain and add. The green berries can be blanched and frozen when in season. Sichuan peppercorns may be substituted.

### Ginger

Add thin slices for antimicrobial action and flavor. Use four or five slices per 2 pounds (1 kg) of pickling bed.

# Making the Pickling Bed

Once you have assembled the ingredients, you'll mix the bed. The following recipe uses just over two pounds (1 kg) of nuka and makes a pickling bed that will fit two to three cucumbers at a time, enough for a family of four for one day. Double or triple the recipe for a large family or one that eats lots of pickles. The recipe requires a container with about a three-quart (3 liter) capacity. If raw nuka is not available, toasted nuka may be used. The amount of water needed will vary depending on the dryness of your nuka and the humidity of your living environment.

**FOR A 3-QUART (3-LITER) CONTAINER**

2¼ lb (1 kg) raw nuka
3⅓ to 4¼ cups (800 ml to 1 liter) water
6 tablespoons (110 g) salt
2 pieces dried kombu, each about 2 in (5 cm) long
2 red chili peppers, seeded and sliced

**Combine the nuka and salt**
**1.** Place the nuka and salt in the pickling container. If there's not enough room to mix in your container, use a large pan or bowl and transfer to your container after step 5.

**Mix well**
**2.** Toss the nuka and salt together by hand. Make sure the salt is evenly distributed.

**Add the water**
**3.** To dissolve the salt more easily, heat the water to lukewarm (about 104°F /40°C). Add 3⅓ cups water in several additions. If using tap water, boil first to remove chlorine, or let sit overnight (see p. 16).

**Mix well**
**4.** Mix with your hands, making sure to moisten all the nuka. Add additional water until the nuka feels like miso. When a handful is squeezed together, it should not crumble and water should drip between your fingers.

**Add the kombu and other flavorings**
**5.** Mix in the kombu and chili. Add any other flavorings now, too (see p. 17).

**Smooth the surface**
**6.** Press the mixture firmly into the container to remove air and flatten the surface. Wipe the nuka off the sides of the container to prevent mold. You're ready to make "throw-away pickles."

# Throw-Away Pickling

A freshly made pickling bed isn't ready to ferment pickles for the table just yet. First you need to do some "throw-away pickling" to help the bed mature. By pickling vegetable scraps, you'll stimulate the microbial activity that promotes fermentation and maturation. The best vegetables to add are daikon radish tops and the outer leaves of cabbage. Leafy greens are particularly effective because they have a lot of moisture and a large surface area, with plenty of lactobacilli attached to them. The key is to mix the bed thoroughly every day, even during the throw-away pickling stage.

For throw-away pickling, use the outermost leaves of leafy vegetables such as cabbage and napa cabbage, yellowed daikon radish leaves and tails, and other scraps.

For a 2 lb (1 kg) pickling bed, bury 1 or 2 outer cabbage leaves in the pickling bed. Mix daily. After 3 to 4 days, discard the old cabbage leaves and add new scraps. Repeat this process 3 or 4 times. When you smell a sour aroma coming from the container, it's a sign that fermentation has progressed. You're ready to pickle for eating!

# Mixing the Pickling Bed

There is a technique to mixing the pickling bed. Oxygen-loving film yeasts tend to form on the surface, while oxygen-hating butyric acid bacteria inhabit the bottom. Too many of either of these microorganisms will spoil the aroma of the pickling bed. To keep them in check, the key is to mix the bed so that the top and bottom switch places. The goal is to move microorganisms that live on the top and bottom of the pickling bed into environments that are unfavorable to them.

As a rule, the bed should be mixed in this way every day, but in the hot summer months, when microorganisms grow faster, it should be mixed every morning and evening. During winter, or if you keep the bed in the refrigerator, it's fine to leave it unmixed for two to three days at a time.

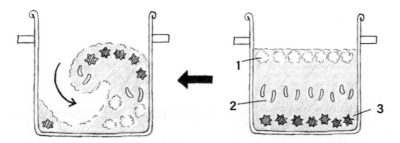

Oxygen-loving yeasts (1) tend to grow on the surface of the pickling bed, while oxygen-hating butyric acid bacteria (3) grow on the bottom. Both should be kept in check. Push the surface mash firmly into the bed, then lift the bottom mash to the surface so the top and bottom are reversed. Since most lactobacilli (2) prefer an environment with little oxygen, end by pressing the top of the bed to release air and flatten the surface, reducing the surface area exposed to oxygen.

# Adding Nuka and Salt to the Pickling Bed

Every day, as you pickle vegetables, the water content of the pickling bed increases and mash clinging to the vegetables is lost. Eventually, you will need to add nuka and salt to the bed. For every two pounds (1 kg) of pickling bed, add a scant cup (100 g) of nuka and 7% of the nuka's weight in salt (about 1 teaspoon). Either raw or toasted nuka is fine, but they have different weights, so weigh them until you get used to adding the salt and nuka. After adding the nuka and salt, mix well to thoroughly blend them into the pickling bed.

Do not pickle vegetables or stir the pickling bed for two to three days. Watch for signs that the bed has matured. When a thin white film of yeast forms on the surface, it is a signal that lactobacilli have increased and you can start pickling vegetables again.

For each 2 lbs (1 kg) of pickling bed, add a scant cup (100 g) of nuka and 7% of the nuka's weight in salt. Kombu and chili peppers can be replenished as needed.

Adding fresh nuka and salt also helps fix a pickling bed that has become too salty or developed an off smell. But be careful not to add salt and nuka too frequently, as this will slow fermentation.

## Chapter 2

# Basic Pickling Instructions

The beauty of nukazuke pickles is that anyone can make a tasty and nutritious dish simply by adding foods to the pickling bed. In addition to favorites like cucumber, eggplant and turnip, many other ingredients such as meat and seafood benefit from the flavor of the pickling bed. In this chapter I explain how to pickle everything from traditional ingredients to unusual but surprisingly addictive new favorites.

# Preparing the Ingredients

Different ingredients require different preparation before you add them to the pickling bed. Don't skip these basic steps for outstanding pickles.

## Vegetables

The key to preparing vegetables is to remove bitterness and other unpleasant flavors before pickling. It is also important to choose fresh, seasonal vegetables.

**Pickle as-is**
For vegetables such as carrots and young turnips that have a mild flavor and can be eaten raw, simply rinse, dry, and add to the bed. Large vegetables may be halved or quartered.

**Parboil**
Vegetables that cannot be eaten raw, such as potato, pumpkin and burdock root, should be parboiled before pickling. Cut to the desired size, boil briefly, drain and cool. **It's important not to overcook the vegetables; they should remain firm.**

**Rub with salt**
For vegetables that might be bitter, such as cucumber and eggplant, rub well with salt before pickling. Leafy vegetables such as radish tops and shungiku (garland chrysanthemum) should also be rubbed with salt until wilted and then squeezed dry.

**Steam**
Steaming is a great way to prepare vegetables such as taro root, new potato and broccoli that are hard but not bitter. Unlike boiling, steaming retains nutritional value and locks in umami.

## Other Methods

**Pre-pickle in salt**
Vegetables with high water content like napa cabbage taste better if they are pre-pickled. In a ziplock bag, massage with about 2% of the vegetable's weight in salt. Let rest for a day or two before adding to the bed.

**Dry**
Mushrooms and daikon radishes should be dried in the sun for six to twelve hours before pickling. This concentrated their umami and increases their nutritional value.

# Fish

Many types of seafood such as mackerel, tuna and squid can be pickled. Seafood that is not sashimi grade should be sprinkled with salt to remove odors, and should be cooked before eating.

Fillet whole fish, sprinkle with salt, and let rest in the refrigerator for an hour or two. Pat dry and place in a ziplock bag with pickling mash to coat. For sashimi-grade fish, there is no need to salt before coating with mash.

# Meat

A variety of meats such as chicken thighs and tenders and pork chops can be marinated with pickling mash. Very little preparation is required. Simply coat with some of the mash from the bed and pickle in a ziplock bag separate from the main pickling bed.

For large pieces of meat such as chicken thighs, score the thicker part of the meat to ensure fast, even pickling.

**It is safest to pickle fish and meat in the refrigerator.** If you use this method, pickling times will be longer than those listed in the instructions. Experiment to find the degree of fermentation you prefer.

# Pickling Vegetables

## Cauliflower

Remove outer leaves, score the thick part of the stem, and break into florets. Be careful not to cut into the florets because they fall apart easily. Parboil, making sure not to overcook, drain, and cool before placing in the pickling bed. Fresh, tender cauliflower may be lightly salted and pickled raw.

▶ Season: winter
▶ Pickling time: 1 day

The pickling times given here assume you keep your pickling bed at room temperature. If you keep yours in the refrigerator, double the pickling times.

Seasonality varies widely by location, so check your local farmers' market to see what's fresh.

## Salad Turnips

Tender and juicy, salad turnips (Asian turnips) are a popular vegetable for nukazuke pickling. In fall they have thicker skins, but the pickling process works wonders on them, so peeling isn't necessary. Pickle smaller turnips whole and cut larger ones in half lengthwise before pickling. Put the tops into the bed with the turnips.

▶ Season: spring and fall
▶ Pickling time: 1 day for roots; 12 hours for tops

A deep cross cut in the bottom of larger turnips ensures even pickling. Massage the tops with a little salt and squeeze to remove moisture before pickling.

## Kabocha Squash

Sweet kabocha squash turns slightly sour when pickled, like a Japanese-style marinated vegetable. Kabocha squash is harvested from late summer to fall, but grows sweeter when stored for several months at room temperature. Pickling the squash around the year's end yields the sweetest results. Kabocha squash is typically parboiled before pickling but if you pare off the skin and slice it thinly, you can sprinkle with salt and add to the pickling bed raw.

▶ Season: late summer to fall
▶ Pickling time: 12 hours in summer; 1 day in fall and winter

Cut into medium-size chunks, remove the seeds, parboil, and cool before pickling. When pickling raw, be sure to ferment until the raw flavor is gone.

## Cabbage

Pickle tender spring cabbage briefly for salad-like results. In winter, when cabbage is crisp and sweet, leave it in the bed longer to bring out its sweetness. Typically, cabbage is split in half or quartered before placing in the bed. Once pickled, the leaves are peeled off to serve. If your container is small, you can pickle individual leaves.

▶ Season: spring through fall
▶ Pickling time: 12 hours in spring; 1½ to 2 days in winter

Halve or quarter before pickling. To encourage even pickling, spread the inner leaves and sprinkle with salt before placing in the bed.

## Cucumber

Cucumber is the iconic summer nukazuke pickle. Because cucumbers have a mild flavor, they absorb the aroma and taste of the pickling bed easily. However, if you only pickle cucumbers and don't salt them first, the pickling bed may become bitter. Pickling sweet vegetables like kabocha squash and carrot together with cucumbers helps maintain a pleasant flavor. Rub cucumbers thoroughly with salt before pickling.

▶ Season: summer
▶ Pickling time: 6 hours

To remove harsh or bitter flavors, cut off both ends, sprinkle with salt, rub well, and dry before adding to the pickling bed. Cucumbers ferment quickly.

## Burdock Root

The umami component of burdock root is found in the skin, so pickle them without peeling. Cut into pieces short enough to eat at one sitting, scrub with a vegetable brush to remove any dirt, and parboil to remove harsh flavors before pickling. The new burdock roots that appear in early summer are very mild, so they are delicious lightly salted and pickled raw. Look for them at Asian grocery stores.

▶ Season: early summer to winter
▶ Pickling time: 1 day in early summer to fall; 1 to 2 days in winter

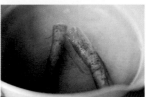

Parboil and let cool before pickling. The roots should remain firm. Cut thick roots in half lengthwise for faster pickling. For attractive pale pickles, blanch first in water with a spoonful of vinegar added.

## Komatsuna Greens

With their mild flavor and sturdy texture, komatsuna greens are among the best greens for nukazuke pickling. They have little bitterness, and their unique umami taste pairs well with the flavor of nukazuke. Lightly pickled komatsuna is refreshingly sour and crunchy, while greens that have been fermented for longer are great stir-fried or added to other dishes. Try substituting tatsoi, bok choy, or Swiss chard.

▶ Season: fall to winter
▶ Pickling time: 1 day in fall; 1½ to 2 days in winter

Lightly salt and massage till limp. Squeeze out moisture before placing in the pickling bed. Blanching is optional but speeds the fermentation process.

## Taro Root

Japanese taro root has a slightly viscous texture, which is enhanced by nukazuke pickling. Peeling the roots and boiling in the starchy water left over from rinsing rice makes a beautiful white pickle with a less viscous texture. Steaming whole with the skins on locks in flavor and nutrients, retains the stickiness, and makes them much easier to peel for pickling.

Steam with skins on until a wooden skewer can be inserted. Peel and cool before pickling. Halve or quarter larger roots.

▸ Season: fall to winter
▸ Pickling time: 12 hours to 1 day in fall; 1 to 1½ days in winter

## Potato

Nukazuke-pickled potatoes have a refreshing umami and sourness, almost like they're coated with sour cream. You can eat them as-is, mash them, or add to potato salad and other dishes. The new potatoes of early summer are ideal for nukazuke because they are tender, mild, and ferment easily, even with the skin on.

---

▶ Season: early summer to fall
▶ Pickling time: 12 hours in early summer to fall; 1 day in winter

---

Steam or boil with the skin on until a wooden skewer can be inserted. Cool before placing in the pickling bed. Halve or quarter larger potatoes.

## Celery

Celery's crunchy texture and distinctive aroma make it a standout among the many types of nukazuke pickles. Pickle lightly to play up its refreshing crunch. The trick to quick pickling is to remove tough strings and score the base. Pickling for too long can make celery stringy. The leaves can be pickled along with the stems.

---

▶ Season: winter to spring
▶ Pickling time: 1 day in winter; 12 hours to 1 day in spring

---

Cut to lengths that fit in the pickling bed. Score the root end with one or two cuts, sprinkle with a pinch of salt, and rub in. Pat dry before pickling.

## Daikon Radish

The leaf end of daikon radishes tends to be sweeter and the tail end spicier, so experiment to see which part you prefer for pickles. For whiter pickles you can peel before pickling, but don't discard the peel—pickle it, too. Drying whole daikon radishes in the sun for a day or so before pickling improves fermentation and yields a sweeter result.

---

▶ Season: fall to winter
▶ Pickling time: 1 day in fall; 1½ to 2 days in winter

---

Cut into chunks small enough to eat in one sitting, slice in half lengthwise, and place in the pickling bed. Sprinkle leaves with salt, massage, and squeeze out moisture before pickling.

## Eggplant

The tricky part about pickling eggplants is retaining their pretty purple color. Some cooks use alum or iron (such as a nail added to the bed), but rubbing eggplants with plenty of salt works best. Careful salting removes acridity and creates a film on the surface that reduces discoloration. Use tender Chinese or Japanese eggplants that have been stored at room temperature. Hard eggplants make hard, tasteless pickles. If you end up with hard pickles, massage thoroughly and rinse in cold water.

---

▶ Season: summer
▶ Pickling time: 6 to 8 hours

---

Rub with plenty of salt and massage until purple juices seep out. Squeeze to remove moisture and place in the bed without rinsing.

*Eggplant changes color when pickled because anthocyanin, a pigment, reacts with the acid produced by lactobacilli. Coating the eggplant with salt suppresses the lactic acid fermentation around the skin and reduces the pigment's reaction with the acid, preventing discoloration. Sprinkle salt on large pieces as soon as they are cut to prevent oxidation and discoloration.

## Carrot

The skin is rich in health-promoting compounds, so I recommend pickling the whole carrot, without peeling. Since the skin tends to darken when pickled, however, you may choose to remove a thin layer before pickling. Hard vegetables like carrots take longer to pickle. To speed the process, lightly sprinkle with salt and rub in before placing in the bed.

▶ Season: summer to early winter
▶ Pickling time: 1 day in summer to fall; 1½ to 2 days in winter

Halve or quarter larger carrots lengthwise for even pickling. To speed fermentation, peel them or rub with salt before placing in the bed.

## Bell Pepper

Red, yellow, and orange bell peppers are sweeter and less bitter than green ones, and work surprisingly well as nukazuke pickles. They are also attractive because they do not fade or discolor when pickled, adding vibrant color to the table. Cut in half before pickling to speed fermentation.

▶ Season: summer to early fall
▶ Pickling time: 12 hours

Cut in half lengthwise and remove the stems and seeds. Rinse and pat dry before placing in the pickling bed.

## Yamaimo Yam

Nukazuke pickling brings out the best in fresh, crispy yamaimo. Cut into lengths short enough to eat in one sitting, burn or scrape off the hairy roots with a knife, and pickle with the skin on. Yamaimo is slimy and can make the pickling bed slimy as well, so it's best pickled separately in a ziplock bag. Scoop out some pickling mash to coat the chunks of yamaimo in the bag.

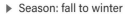

▸ Season: fall to winter
▸ Pickling time: 1 day in fall; 1½ to 2 days in winter

Remove the hair-like roots on yamaimo yams by either scraping with a knife or singeing over a gas burner, taking care not to burn your hands. Don't peel before pickling.

## Lotus Root

To make the color of lotus root more vibrant, parboil it in hot water with a splash of vinegar until it can be pierced with a wooden skewer. Freshly harvested lotus root, available from late summer to early fall, has a tender, crunchy texture and can be pickled raw. The skin and ends are rich in health-promoting compounds, so be sure not to peel.

▸ Season: summer to winter
▸ Pickling time: 12 hours in summer; 1 day in fall and winter

Halve or quarter lengthwise and parboil with the skin on, adding a dash of vinegar to the water. Drain and cool before placing in the pickling bed.

# Other Vegetables to Pickle

Most vegetables can be fermented in your pickling bed, except those that are extremely bitter or aromatic. Experiment with different seasonal vegetables to find your favorites.

### Asparagus
Snap off tough ends, parboil, and cool before pickling. Tender, freshly harvested asparagus and thin stalks may be pickled raw.

▸ Season: spring to early summer
▸ Pickling time: 1 day

### Green Beans
Remove tops and strings, parboil and cool before pickling. Green beans discolor if pickled for too long, so take them out as soon as the pickling time is up.

▸ Season: early summer
▸ Pickling time: 12 hours

### Okra
Salt lightly and roll firmly on a cutting board to massage and remove surface hairs. Place in the pickling bed raw. Cut off the tough tops after pickling. The shorter the pickling time, the brighter the color.

▸ Season: summer
▸ Pickling time: 10 to 12 hours

### Pickling Melon
Called *uri* in Japanese, these not-sweet members of the melon family include chayote and many other favorites for pickling. Peel and halve or quarter. Scoop out the seeds and pickle raw.

▸ Season: summer
▸ Pickling time: 12 hours to 1 day

### Young Ginger
Young ginger is milder and less fibrous than the ginger available year round. Carefully wash off any dirt in the crevices and cut into pieces for pickling. Longer pickling improves the flavor. You can leave ginger in the pickling bed for 6 months to a year, as it imparts its anti-bacterial qualities to the bed.

▸ Season: summer to fall
▸ Pickling time: 3 to 4 days

### Udo
The shoots that emerge from this wild perennial plant (*Aralia cordata*) in spring are deliciously crisp. Cut to fit in the pickling bed, peel thickly, and soak in vinegar water for several hours to remove bitterness. Pat dry and pickle raw. The leaves and buds can be handled the same way.

▸ Season: spring
▸ Pickling time: 12 hours to 1 day

## Zucchini

Slice off the stem end, which can be bitter, and the tail end. Sprinkle lightly with salt, rub in, and halve lengthwise. Pickle raw. Cut longer zucchini to fit the pickling bed.

▶ Season: summer
▶ Pickling time: 12 hours

## Bamboo Shoot

Boil fresh bamboo shoots, sheath on, in plenty of water with a cup of nuka and 1 chili pepper until tender, about 1 hour. Leave in the water overnight. The next day, rinse, peel and cut in halves, quarters or eighths before pickling. Alternately, buy prepared fresh shoots at an Asian grocery (but avoid canned ones).

▶ Season: spring
▶ Pickling time: 12 hours

## Malabar Spinach

Sprinkle lightly with salt, rub in and let stand until wilted. Thoroughly squeeze out the moisture and place in the pickling bed. It is best not to pickle for too long because the leaves will become very slimy.

▶ Season: summer
▶ Pickling time: 6 to 8 hours

## Seri

Seri (*Oenanthe javanica*) is a Japanese herb with a delicate fragrance, often eaten blanched. Sprinkle lightly with salt, let sit until wilted, then thoroughly squeeze out moisture before pickling. To preserve the fresh aroma, a short pickling time is best.

▶ Season: spring
▶ Pickling time: 12 hours

## Nanohana (Brassica Blossoms)

Nanohana are the spring blossoms of field mustard. If you have a garden, you can substitute other members of the brassica family that have bolted. Choose those with tightly closed buds. Sprinkle lightly with salt, massage, and thoroughly squeeze out moisture before pickling. You can also pre-pickle with a pinch of salt in a ziplock bag.

▶ Season: spring
▶ Pickling time: 12 hours to 1 day

## Napa Cabbage

Halve or quarter and sprinkle lightly with salt. Place in a large ziplock bag, press out the air, and place a weight on top such as a pan with a rock or jar of water set inside. Pre-pickle in this way for 1 to 2 days. Thoroughly squeeze out the moisture and transfer to the pickling bed.

▶ In season...Winter
▶ Pickling time: 1 to 1½ days

## Fuki

Use only the stalks of this common wild edible plant, called butterbur (*Petasites japonica*) in English, discarding the leaves. Sprinkle lightly with salt, roll firmly on a cutting board, and parboil. Immediately plunge into cold water, drain and pickle. Remove the fibrous strings after pickling.

▶ Season: spring
▶ Pickling time: 12 hours to 1 day

## Broccoli

Cut into bite sized florets, parboil, and cool before pickling. The thick stems can be halved, peeled, and pickled raw. For quicker pickling, parboil the stems before pickling.

▶ Season: fall and winter
▶ Pickling time: 1 day

## Radish

Lightly sprinkle with salt and massage, leaving the leaves on if they are fresh. When the leaves have wilted, squeeze out the moisture and pickle. Radishes tend to fade when pickled, so be sure to rub the salt in well to preserve their vibrant color.

▶ Season: spring, fall and winter
▶ Pickling time: 12 hours in spring and fall; 1 day in winter

## Mizuna Greens

For larger, more mature bunches of mizuna, remove the base and wash leaves well to remove dirt. Young mizuna can be pickled whole, with the base attached. Sprinkle lightly with salt and let rest until wilted. Squeeze thoroughly to remove moisture before pickling.

▶ In season...Winter
▶ Pickling time...1 day

## Myoga (Japanese Ginger)

The buds of the myoga plant have a delicious fragrance and a pleasant texture. Score the buds lengthwise to encourage even pickling. To preserve the crunchy texture and bright pink color, pickle for a short time.

▶ Season: summer and fall
▶ Pickling time: 12 hours to 1 day in summer; 1 to 1½ days in fall

## Warabi (Bracken Fiddleheads)

Widely eaten in Asia, this wild edible plant is often avoided in the West due to health concerns. Snap off the tough lower stems. Place in a large pot and pour boiling water over to cover. Add about 1 teaspoon of baking soda per quart (liter) of water. Submerge with a plate and leave overnight. The next day, rinse in cold water, drain and pickle.

▶ In Season: spring
▶ Pickling time: 6 hours

# Pickling Seafood and Meat

## Saba (Mackerel)

Nukazuke pickles made from fatty mackerel are refreshing, odorless, and have a deep umami flavor. Once pickled, the fish is best simply grilled. Other oily fish such as sardines, Pacific saury (*sanma*) and yellowtail can be fermented in the same way (see page 25 for preparation instructions).

▶ Season: fall to winter
▶ Pickling time: 1 day

Fillet the fish, remove any remaining bones, and sprinkle with salt. Coat the fillet evenly with pickling mash and place in a ziplock bag. Press out the air and seal.

## Maguro (Bluefin Tuna)

The transformation of a block of sashimi-grade tuna in the pickling bed is rather amazing. The fish takes on a deeper flavor, almost becoming a different food altogether. The pickled tuna works equally well served Japanese-style or in European dishes such as carpaccio. Pickle for a short time to preserve the flavor.

▸ Season: year round
▸ Pickling time: 12 hours

Coat the entire block of tuna with pickling mash and place in a ziplock bag. Press out the air and seal.

## Shrimp

Shrimp can be fermented raw in pickling mash. Remove the shell and devein before pickling; the tail can be left on. Pickled shrimp is delicious simply grilled, or stir-fried with vegetables. Shrimp that have fermented for a longer time and become sour work well in Southeast Asian dishes such as Thai fresh spring rolls.

▸ Season: year round
▸ Pickling time: 12 hours to 1 day

Remove the shell and devein. Wash, sprinkle lightly with salt, and let sit in the refrigerator for an hour or two. Blot dry, coat with pickling mash, and place in a ziplock bag. Press out the air and seal.

## Squid

Fresh squid is pickled raw. Try to find tender whole, sashimi-grade squid at a good fishmonger. Once pickled, enjoy raw or cooked. The side fins and tentacles can also be pickled.

- ▶ Season: year round
- ▶ Pickling time: 12 hours to 1 day

Cut open the body and pull on the tentacles to remove them along with the guts. Peel off the skin, rinse the flesh well and cut in 2 or 3 pieces. Wipe dry, coat with pickling mash, and place in a ziplock bag. Press out the air and seal.

## Octopus

Pickle octopus that is boiled, not raw. After pickling, cut the octopus into bite-size pieces and serve as-is. Octopus is usually quite chewy, but thanks to the action of the lactobacilli in the pickling bed, it becomes soft and tender after fermentation.

- ▶ Season: summer
- ▶ Pickling time: 12 hours to 1 day

Cut boiled tentacles into lengths small enough to eat at one sitting. Coat with pickling mash and place in a ziplock bag. Press out the air and seal.

## Chicken Wings

Pickled chicken wings taste great simply grilled or pan-fried. They have a satisfyingly full flavor even without additional seasoning. Or try stewing the meat with root vegetables such as daikon radish and burdock root. There's no need to wash off the pickling mash before stewing. The meat will be tender and juicy.

▸ Season: year round
▸ Pickling time: 1 day

Coat each chicken wing with pickling mash and place in a ziplock bag. Press out the air and seal.

## Chicken Thighs

The action of lactobacilli in the pickling bed neutralizes the slight gaminess of chicken and makes the meat moist and tender. These pickled thighs can by cooked in the same ways as regular chicken thighs. Grilling, sautéing, deep-frying, and stewing with vegetables all work well.

▸ Season: year round
▸ Pickling time: 1 day

Cut thighs into two or three pieces. Coat the meat evenly with pickling mash and place in a ziplock bag. Press out the air and seal. Cook fully after pickling.

# Unusual Pickles

## Avocado

Avocado is among the most popular novelty items to pickle as nukazuke. It develops a deliciously rich flavor. Fully ripe avocados tend to fall apart in the pickling bed, so use firm avocados and pickle them separately in a ziplock bag. The skin may have wax or pesticide residue on it, so it's best to peel avocado before pickling, although the color will be less attractive.

▶ Season: year round
▶ Pickling time: 1 to 2 days

Cut in half and remove the pit. Peel, coat with pickling mash and place in a ziplock bag. Press out the air and seal.

## Shiitake Mushroom

Fresh shiitake mushrooms are a perfect match for nukazuke. Pickling concentrates their umami and deepens their flavor. They can be placed in the pickling bed as-is, but drying them in the sun for 2 to 3 hours before pickling enhances their umami flavor. Trim the tough bottom of the stem and place in the pickling bed with the stem still attached. After pickling, shiitake mushrooms can be eaten raw.

▶ Season: spring and fall
▶ Pickling time: 1 day

Wipe clean and place in the pickling bed as-is, or dry in the sun first to concentrate the flavor.

## Other Mushrooms

In addition to fresh shiitake mushrooms, king oyster mushrooms, enoki mushrooms, and shimeji mushrooms all work well as nukazuke pickles. Enoki and shimeji mushrooms tend to break apart in the pickling bed, so it is best to tuck them into a large tea bag or wrap in cheesecloth before placing in the bed. They will need to be pickled a little longer than other mushrooms. Once pickled, they can be eaten raw. They are also delicious stir-fried and drizzled with soy sauce.

▶ Season: fall
▶ Pickling time: 1 day

Drying fresh mushrooms in the sun in a well-ventilated place for 2 to 12 hours will remove excess moisture and concentrate the flavor, resulting in a more delicious pickle.

## Fava Bean

Pickled fava beans are a must-try in early summer. The sweetness of the beans paired with the sourness of the pickling bed results in a refreshing flavor that can only be enjoyed in season. Because they are small and tend to get lost in the pickling bed, it is best to place them in a large tea bag or wrap in cheesecloth before pickling. The lactobacilli soften the skins, so you don't need to remove them before eating.

▶ Season: early summer
▶ Pickling time: 12 hours

Remove from the pods and parboil with a pinch of salt. Drain and cool. Pickle with the skins on.

## Onion

Pickle raw onions whole. To serve, slice off the root end and peel off one layer at a time with a knife. If you are concerned about the odor contaminating the main pickling bed, you can pickle them separately in a ziplock bag. The sweet young onions that are available from spring to early summer work especially well as pickles because they are less pungent.

▶ Season: spring to early summer and fall
▶ Pickling time: 2 to 3 days in spring and summer; 4 to 5 days in fall

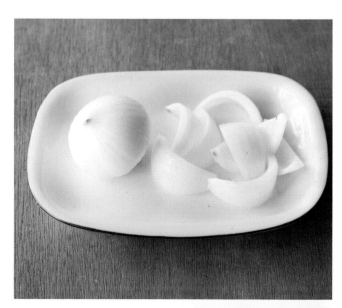

Remove the papery skin and pickle whole. For larger onions or to speed fermentation, halve or quarter lengthwise with the root end attached.

## Cherry Tomato

Large tomatoes are too soft and moist for pickling, but cherry tomatoes work. Since their firm skin slows fermentation, it is best to cut one or two thin slits in the skin before pickling. Avoid fully ripe, soft tomatoes, as they tend to be crushed in the pickling bed.

▶ Season: summer
▶ Pickling time: 12 hours

## Persimmon

The mild, rich sweetness of persimmon turns into a refreshing aftertaste when pickled. Persimmons also add sweetness to the pickling bed itself. There's no need to peel before serving since fermentation softens the skin. Fully ripe fruit tends to be crushed in the pickling bed, so choose firm, slightly under-ripe Fuyu (not Hachiya) persimmons.

▶ Season: fall
▶ Pickling time: 12 hours to 1 day

Halve or quarter and pickle with the skin on. After pickling, slice into bite-size pieces.

## Apple

The sweetness of apples balanced with a hint of sourness and saltiness is a delicacy unique to nukazuke pickling. Brief pickling preserves the flavor and vibrant color of apples. The skin contains many health-promoting components, so if your apples are organic, pickle them with their skins on.

▸ Season: fall to winter
▸ Pickling time: 12 hours to 1 day

Halve or quarter and pickle with the skin on, then slice before serving. If you are concerned about pesticide residue, peel before pickling.

## Kiriboshi Daikon

Kiriboshi daikon, or dried shredded daikon radish, is sold at Asian grocery stores and has a natural sweetness that goes well with the sourness of nukazuke pickling. Soaking the dried radish strips in water to soften them leaches out their umami, so do not soak them—pickle them dry. As they absorb moisture in the bed, they will also absorb flavor. Pickling kiriboshi daikon is a useful way to reduce the moisture content in a pickling bed that has become too wet and loose.

▸ Season: year round
▸ Pickling time: 1 day

Since kiriboshi daikon tends to get lost in the pickling bed, it should be placed in a large tea bag or wrapped in cheesecloth before pickling. It is best added to the pickling bed dry, without pre-soaking in water as is typical when cooking kiriboshi daikon.

# Dried Kombu

Kombu, a type of kelp, is soaked in water or simmered to make dashi, the stock used daily in Japanese cooking. Instead of discarding the rehydrated kombu from stock-making, you can pickle it. Pickling amplifies the already intense umami flavor of kombu and gives it a smoother texture. The variety called Hidaka kombu works especially well. Dried kombu added to flavor the pickling bed can also be eaten once it has softened, as long as you add new kombu to replace it.

▸ Season: year round
▸ Pickling time: 12 hours to 1 day

## Soybeans

With their hint of sourness, pickled soybeans are addictively tasty. Boil or steam before pickling. If the pickling bed becomes too wet and loose, dry soybeans can be added to absorb moisture, but they are not edible raw. Be sure to cook them before eating. Since soybeans are small, they should be placed in a tea bag before pickling or pickled separately in a ziplock bag with some of the pickling mash.

▶ Season: year round
▶ Pickling time: 1 day

Wash soybeans well and soak overnight in plenty of water. Gently simmer or steam until tender (1 to 2 hours) before pickling.

## Egg

The moderate saltiness and unique smoky aroma of pickled eggs is exquisite. Whether sliced into a salad or added to tartar sauce, they contribute an unusual flavor. Pickled eggs make a tasty snack to serve with drinks as well. Since the eggs are boiled, shelled, and pickled whole, the yolks can be soft set.

▶ Season: year round
▶ Pickling time: 1 day

Boil and shell the eggs before pickling whole.

## Cheese

The combination of two fermented foods—cheese and nukazuke pickles—makes for a delicious marriage. Any type of cheese works well. Try Camembert or Gouda, or experiment with different flavors and textures. Soft, high-moisture cheeses such as mozzarella should be pickled separately from the main bed in a ziplock bag.

▶ Season: year round
▶ Pickling time: 1 day

## Tofu

Pickled tofu has a rich, cheese-like flavor with sour and salty notes. It can be served with rice, as a snack, or blended into a dip. Use firm tofu and press to remove water. Pickle in a ziplock bag with some of the pickling mash. If you put overly moist tofu in the main pickling bed, it may spoil the bed.

▶ Season: year round
▶ Pickling time: 1 day

Wrap firm or medium tofu in cloth, place a weight such as a bowl of water on top, and let stand 2 to 3 hours. Drain well and pickle separately in a ziplock bag.

# More Unusual Pickles

The unusual foods on this page also make excellent nukazuke pickles.
Give them a try and you may discover unexpected delicacies!

### Salted Horse Mackerel

Salted dried horse mackerel, called *aji no himono* in Japanese, is available in the refrigerator or freezer section of some Japanese grocery stores. Coat with pickling mash and place in a ziplock bag. Press out air and seal.

▸ Season: year round
▸ Pickling time: 1 day

### Green Ume

Unripe ume (Japanese apricot) contains trace amounts of amygdalin, a harmful compound, but is safe to eat when pickled. Order online or check Asian grocery stores in season. Wash, dry, and pickle. The fruits are ready to eat when they become translucent.

▸ Season: early summer
▸ Pickling time: 1 week or more

### Small Melons

Cut off a small slice from the top and bottom and pickle whole. Cut larger melons in half lengthwise and remove the seeds before pickling.

▸ Season: summer
▸ Pickling time: 1 day

### Dried Persimmon

Dried persimmons, a traditional Japanese snack available at Asian groceries, can be pickled whole. Cut large persimmons in half lengthwise and remove the pits.

▸ Season: winter
▸ Pickling time: 1 to 2 days

### Garlic

Divide into cloves and peel. The longer they are pickled, the tastier they will be, but be careful not to put too many in the bed or their odor will contaminate it.

▸ Season: early summer
▸ Pickling time: 1 week plus

### Watermelon Rind

The outer rind is tough, so pare it off and cut the juicy inner rind into pieces to pickle. The flavor is similar to cucumber.

▸ Season: summer
▸ Pickling time: 4 to 5 hours

## Chapter 3

# A Nukazuke Pickling Calendar and a Troubleshooting Guide

These days most foods are available year round, but vegetables and fish are still tastiest and healthiest when they're in season. The same goes for nukazuke pickles. In this chapter, you'll find a calendar of pickling ingredients to enjoy in each season and tips for handling the problems you may encounter when you give nukazuke pickling a try.

# A Nukazuke Pickling Calendar

Pickling fresh vegetables in season is the secret to delicious nukazuke pickles. Why not relish the changing seasons through the type of pickles you have on your dining table?
Note: This calendar reflects Japanese growing seasons. Use your local farmer's market as a guide to what grows in your region.

## Early March to Late April

**Bamboo shoot**
Fresh bamboo shoots are in season from mid-March to May. Moso bamboo is most common in Japan. (Page 36)

**Fuki**
Also available from fall to early spring, but the peak of the natural season is from March to May. (Page 37)

**Asparagus**
The season for green asparagus grown outside is from April to early summer. (Page 35)

**Radish**
Available in markets year round, but best in spring and fall. (Page 37)

## Late April to Early May

**Warabi (Bracken fiddleheads)**
Warabi, a quintessential edible wild plant, is in season from March through early summer, depending on location. (Page 37)

**Fava Bean**
Fava beans are in season from late spring through early summer. (Page 46)

**Pickling Melons**
The season for pickling melons and winter melons suitable for pickling is early summer, although more mature melons remain on the market through fall. (Page 35)

## The Spring Pickling Bed
The temperatures at this time of year are optimal for nukazuke pickling. It's also an ideal time to start a new bed.

*Page numbers refer to the pickling instructions for each item.

## Early May to Late June

### Green Ume (Japanese Apricot)
Several varieties are available, all in season in May and June. (Page 52)

### Cucumber
The classic nukazuke pickle, cucumber season starts in June and peaks in high summer. (Page 28)

### Green Bean
A summer vegetable with a long season running from June to September. (Page 35)

### Malabar Spinach
Vibrant, fresh Malabar spinach is available from June or July through fall. (Page 36)

### Myoga (Japanese Ginger)
Summer myoga is available around June, and fall myoga around September. (Page 37)

## Late June to Early July

### Zucchini
Zucchini season starts in June and spans the summer. Use young, firm zucchini for pickling. (Page 37)

### Kabocha Squash
The main season is from midsummer to fall, although they can be stored for winter eating. (Page 27)

### Sardine
The season varies depending on region and species, but in general, fresh sardines are caught from July through fall.

### Okra
Bright green okra are in season from June to September. (Page 35)

## Early July to late August

### Eggplant
There are many varieties of eggplant, from round to long to egg-shaped, but most are in season from midsummer to fall. (Page 32)

### Bell pepper
Bell peppers of all colors are in season from midsummer through fall. (Page 33)

## The Summer Pickling Bed
Temperatures above 86°F (30°C) on consecutive days can cause abnormal fermentation. Move the bed to a cooler place such as a refrigerator.

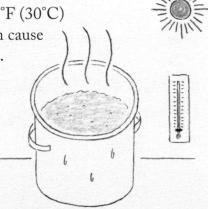

## Late August to Early September

**Persimmon**
The harvest begins in September and peaks from October to November. The firm-fleshed Fuyu variety is used for pickling. (Page 47)

**Taro Root**
Depending on the variety, the season is generally from late summer to winter. Stores well. (Page 30)

**Young Ginger**
The season for greenhouse grown young ginger is summer. Young ginger grown outside is available starting in late October. (Page 35)

**Sanma (Pacific Saury)**
The fattiest, tastiest sanma swim southwards in the Sea of Japan in September and October.

**Salmon**
Available year-round, but best in fall when wild salmon swim upriver from the ocean to spawn.

## Early September to Late October

**Carrot**
Harvested in different regions year round, but those picked from September onward have the most nutrients and are best for pickling. (Page 33)

# The Fall Pickling Bed

Fall has ideal ambient temperatures for the pickling bed, between 68° and 77°F (20° to 25°C), enabling proper fermentation and delicious pickles.

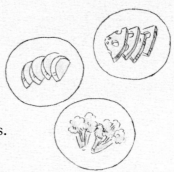

## Late October to Early November

**Salad Turnip**
Small, tender turnips are in season from November to December and again in spring. (Page 27)

**Burdock Root**
Some are harvested young in summer, but the peak season is from November on. (Page 29)

**Yamaimo Yam**
The spring harvest takes place in April and May and the fall harvest in November and December. (Page 34)

**Napa Cabbage**
In season starting in November and tastiest from then until February. (Page 36)

**Cauliflower**
Available year round, but most delicious from November to early spring. (Page 26)

**Lotus Root**
Starts to appear in markets around October and becomes gradually more nutritious as winter progresses. (Page 34)

**Late November to Early December**

**Broccoli**
Reliably available year round, but at its best from November through March. (Page 37)

**Komatsuna Greens**
The dark leafy greens withstand frost well and are tastiest from December to March. (Page 29)

**Early December to Late January**

**Mizuna Greens**
In season throughout winter and early spring. (Page 37)

**Daikon Radish**
Daikon radish is available year-round, but the season for the popular type that's tinted green at the top runs from November to February. (Page 32)

**Late January to Early February**

**Seri (*Oenanthe javanica*)**
The outdoor season starts in February; available from greenhouses a bit earlier. (Page 36)

**Nanohana (Brassica Blossoms)**
The edible blossoms of field mustard are in season from February to April. Other plants in the brassica family blossom at various times of the year. (Page 36)

---

**Early February to Late March**

**New Potato**
The harvest starts in early March in southern and western Japan. The skins are thin then and the potatoes have a high moisture content. (Page 31)

**Spring Cabbage**
Although cabbage is in season in various regions in summer and winter, spring cabbage is the sweetest and most tender. (Page 28)

**Celery**
Available year round but in season in spring, starting in March. (Page 31)

**Udo (*Aralia cordata*)**
Available from greenhouses starting in December and peaking in March. Udo grown outside is in season around May. (Page 35)

## The Winter Pickling Bed

When temperatures drop, fermentation immediately slows. You can skip mixing the pickling bed for 2 to 3 days at a time in winter.

# A Troubleshooting Guide

The nukazuke pickling bed is alive. The taste of the foods you pickle in it will vary depending on how you care for it. Learning more about the bed and how to nurture it will help you make more flavorful pickles with the specific taste you want.

## Preparing the Pickling Bed

**Q1. Plastic containers are readily available. Can I use them for pickling?**

**A1. Plastic containers labeled "food grade" can be used for pickling. The salt and lactic acid in the pickling bed will not degrade the plastic.** Depending on the container, however, a plasticky smell may be transferred to the pickling bed and vegetables. Some inexpensive plastic containers are not resistant to acid and salt, and are easily damaged.

    I recommend enamel, ceramic, or glass containers because they are odor- and leak-proof, acid- and salt-resistant, do not leach chemical substances, and do not affect the flavor or quality of the food in them. They must have lids to keep insects and dust out. Wooden barrels are ideal pickling containers because they are well ventilated and absorb a moderate amount of moisture, but they are susceptible to excessive drying out, odor leakage, and insect infestation, making them a better choice for experienced nukazuke pickle makers who can keep a close eye on them.

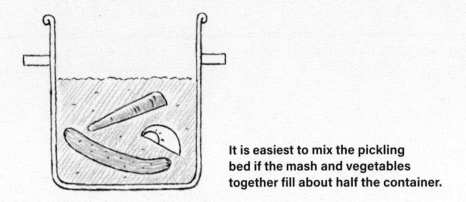

**It is easiest to mix the pickling bed if the mash and vegetables together fill about half the container.**

## Q2. What shape should the container be?

**A2. I recommend a cylindrical container big enough to hold at least three times the amount of nuka used.** This type of container makes it easy to reach every corner when mixing and has a relatively small surface area exposed to oxygen.

If you don't have the space to store a cylindrical container, you can use a shallow rectangular container. However, since mixing the bed in a shallow container is difficult, I suggest removing all the vegetables from the pickling bed prior to mixing, then replacing when you're done.

## Q3. It's hard for me to get fresh raw nuka. What should I do?

**A3.** Nuka is the key to nukazuke pickles. It is best to use freshly milled raw nuka, available from rice producers or specialty shops online.

**If raw nuka is not available, toasted nuka is readily available online or can be purchased from Asian grocery stores and some natural food stores.** The vitamins and enzymes in raw nuka are easily destroyed by heat, slowing fermentation, but toasting prevents the growth of bacteria and insects and extends the shelf life of nuka.

### Q4. How long will raw nuka last if I can't use it all at once?

**A4.** Because nuka has a high fat content, it oxidizes quickly. Also, pesticide-free or low-pesticide raw nuka is more likely to attract insects. **Try to use nuka from freshly milled rice as soon as possible, within 3 to 4 days at most.** If you want to keep it longer, put it in an airtight bag, press out the air and freeze it. It should remain usable for 2 to 3 months with no change in quality. You can also toast it before freezing.

### Q5. Should I add kombu and chili peppers to the bed regularly?

**A5.** Kombu adds umami to the bed and chili peppers prevent mold and oxidation. You may remove the kombu to eat it, or inadvertently remove chilies when taking out your pickles. **Both should be added when they run out, so that they are always present in the pickling bed.**

### Q6. The bed is not fermenting well and pickling is slow.

**A6.** The optimum temperature for a nukazuke pickling bed is around 68° to 77°F (20°–25°C). Temperatures below this suppress lactobacilli activity and slow fermentation. **Move the pickling bed to a warmer place, or bury a plastic bottle filled with body-temperature water in the bed to warm it.**

Pickling will also not be successful if the bed is too dry. When you squeeze a handful of pickling mash, water should drip from between your fingers. **Add water as necessary.**

Sometimes the pickling bed benefits from resting in order to activate the lactobacilli. Remove all the vegetables and leave the bed at room temperature for about 3 days to reduce the oxygen supply. After that, mix thoroughly and start pickling again. Avoid doing this in summer.

## Daily Care of the Pickling Bed

### Q7. Do I really have to mix the pickling bed every day?

**A7. Generally, you need to mix the pickling bed once or twice a day to feed it oxygen.** This suppresses the growth of bacteria that don't like oxygen (anaerobic bacteria) and stimulates the activity of yeasts that likes oxygen (aerobic yeasts). If your container is unventilated plastic or enamel, it is especially important to mix the bed every day.

If you prefer a longer pickling time because you don't eat pickles every day, or if you can't mix the pickling bed daily, you can keep it in the refrigerator. At low temperatures fermentation slows and the growth of bacteria is suppressed, so even if you don't mix the bed every day it is less likely to be damaged. However, after a prolonged period in the refrigerator the activity of lactobacilli inevitably weakens and your pickles will become less flavorful. For this reason, it's a good idea to move your pickling bed to room temperature from time to time.

### Q8. Do I have to mix the pickling bed with my bare hands? I don't want my hands to get smelly.

**A8.** If you mix the bed with rubber gloves on every day, the smell of the rubber may transfer to the pickling bed. In addition, lactobacilli are present on our hands, and I feel that mixing with bare hands transfers these lactobacilli to the bed, creating a taste that is unique to you. **I encourage you to mix the bed with your bare hands.**

If you have a cut or other wound, the salt from the bed will be painful, so wear gloves or have someone else do the mixing for you.

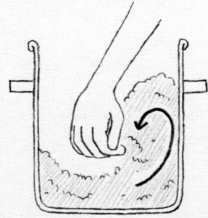

**If possible, mix the pickling bed with bare hands. You will be able to get a direct sense for the condition of the bed, such as its moisture and texture.**

### Q9. My pickling bed has become somewhat "loose." Should I drain off the moisture?

**A9.** The pickling mash should be just moist enough for liquid to seep between your fingers when you squeeze it. If the bed becomes wetter than that, it tends to over-ferment, so **add new nuka and salt (about 7% by weight of the nuka that you add).** You can also add dried shiitake mushrooms, kiriboshi daikon (shredded dried radish), or soybeans to soak up excess moisture. Remove when they are rehydrated. The rehydrated mushrooms and daikon can be enjoyed as-is, but be sure to boil the soybeans before serving. The excess liquid in the bed is packed with the flavor and nutrients of vegetables, so don't soak it up with paper towels and throw it away.

### Q10. There is a strange smell coming from the pickling bed. What is the cause?

**A10. A sharp, paint-thinner-like odor is caused by film yeast.** When this aerobic microorganism grows too vigorously, it produces a strong odor. **If you smell something like dirty socks, there is too much anaerobic butyric acid bacteria at the bottom of the bed.**

Both are caused by insufficient mixing. Mix the pickling bed to move the oxygen-loving yeast to the bottom and the oxygen-hating butyric acid bacteria to the surface. By moving them to a less hospitable environment, the growth of both can be suppressed.

It is also important to adjust the moisture content of the pickling bed. Too little moisture causes a pungent odor and too much causes a putrid smell.

**Don't panic if you discover mold growing on the pickling bed. Just remove the moldy part and your bed will be fine.**

## Mold in the Pickling Bed

**Q11. Black or blue mold is growing on top of the pickling bed! Do I have to throw away the whole bed?**

**A11.** If black, blue, red, or other colors of mold appear, **remove the mold immediately.** Scrape off about half an inch (1 cm) of the pickling mash below the mold with a spoon or similar tool. **You do not need to discard the entire bed.**

**Q12. I have noticed a white mold-like substance on the surface of my pickling bed. Should I remove it?**

**A12.** If there is a faint white film on the surface, it is film yeast. On the surface of the pickling bed, where it is in contact with oxygen, film yeast emits a strange odor. Lower down, in the absence of oxygen, it produces alcohol and fatty acids, the source of a pickling bed's typical mellow aroma. Film yeasts also eat excessive lactobacilli, preventing the bed from becoming too sour. **If the bed is only faintly covered with white film, mixing the film in will enhance the unique flavor of the nuka.**

However, if the film yeast grows too much, it will emit an odor like paint thinner that assaults your nose and degrades the flavor of the pickles. If a white film covers the entire surface of the bed, remove it with a spoon and add new nuka and salt (about 7% of the weight of the nuka you're adding). After adding the nuka and salt, let the bed rest for several days to promote the growth of lactic acid bacteria before you start pickling again.

## Storing the Pickling Bed

**Q13. Where should I store the pickling bed?**

**A13.** The ideal location has a year-round temperature of about 68° to 77°F (20° to 25°C). Underfloor storage is ideal, but since this is often not possible, **I recommend keeping the bed in a cool, well-ventilated location in summer and in a warmer location in winter.** Avoid places that are too hot or fluctuate widely in temperature, such as near gas stoves, microwave ovens, or heating vents. If your kitchen is too small to accommodate the pickling bed, you can place it on a balcony or in the garden, as long as it is not exposed to direct sunlight or rain.

**Q14. Do I need to cover the picking bed with a dish towel, or place weights on it?**

**A14. I don't recommend using a dish towel** because bacteria on the cloth can cause the pickling bed to become moldy. Covering the container with a lid is enough. Also, because the pickling bed contains salt, the vegetables will dehydrate naturally, meaning **there is no need to place weights on the bed.**

**Q15. Can I store the pickling container in the refrigerator in summer?**

**A15. The pickling bed is normally kept at room temperature, but may be placed in the refrigerator when room temperatures exceed 86°F (30°C).** At these temperatures, lactobacilli ferment abnormally. They may become too sour or even die.

However, since placing the pickling bed in the refrigerator slows the activity of the lactobacilli and delays the pickling process, be sure to wait until your bed is mature and producing tasty pickles before putting it the refrigerator. Do not leave it in the refrigerator permanently. When the weather cools, return it to room temperature.

### Q16. What should I do if I will be away for 1 to 2 weeks?

**A16. Remove all the pickled vegetables, spread new nuka on the surface, and sprinkle with salt weighing 7% of the newly added nuka.** If the temperature is above 86°F (30°C), place in the refrigerator; if below that, place in a cool, well-ventilated place. When you return home, just mix it and start pickling again.

### Q17. I want to store the bed for a long time without pickling anything. Can I freeze it?

**A17.** If you are going on a long trip or want to take a break during winter, freeze the pickling bed. **Take out all the vegetables and freeze the pickling mash.** If you can't fit the whole container in the freezer, transfer the mash to a ziplock bag, press out the air, seal tightly, and place in the freezer. When you take it out, the microorganisms will wake from their dormant state and you can use the bed as before.

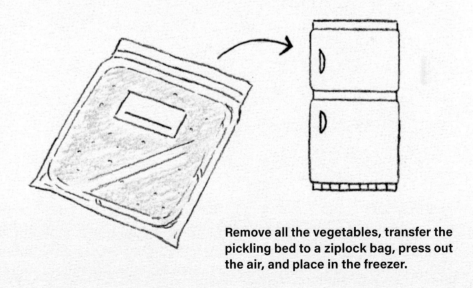

**Remove all the vegetables, transfer the pickling bed to a ziplock bag, press out the air, and place in the freezer.**

## Improving the Quality of Your Nukazuke Pickles

### Q18. The pickles are too sour! What can I do?

**A18. Mix the bed thoroughly once or twice a day, making sure to reverse the position of the pickling mash on the top and bottom of the bed.** Lactobacilli prefer an oxygen-poor environment. If you don't aerate the bed often enough by mixing it, they will multiply and produce a lot of lactic acid, which causes a sour taste.

If temperatures are high, move the pickling bed to as cool a place as possible. The optimum temperature for lactobacilli in nuka is 68° to 77°F (20° to 25°C). A temperature above this will produce more acid. Adding a little salt also helps. Salt inhibits the growth of lactobacilli.

Another method is to add eggshells, because their calcium neutralizes acid. Crush the shells before adding to the pickling bed. The shells of raw eggs may harbor salmonella bacteria, so it is best to boil the eggs before shelling.

**Peel boiled eggs, remove the thin inner skin, and break the shell into small pieces before adding to the pickling bed.**

### Q19. The pickles are too salty. What can I do?

**A19.** The bed's salt content may become too high because of the salt you sprinkle on vegetables before pickling. This weakens the activity of many lactobacilli in the pickling bed and causes the salty taste to overpower the sour taste. **Lower the salt concentration by adding new nuka.** The pickling bed should taste slightly salty when you sample it.

## Q20. My pickled eggplants and cucumbers are discolored and unattractive. How can I make the colors brighter?

**A20.** One method is to put rusted nails or chunks of iron in the pickling bed, but this will cause other vegetables to darken and discolor. An easier, more effective method is to firmly rub cucumbers and eggplant with salt before pickling.

**Rub a generous amount of salt on eggplants and massage firmly until purple juice oozes out.** Squeeze thoroughly to remove excess moisture and place in the pickling bed. To prevent their color from staining the rest of the bed, avoid moving the eggplants once you've buried them in the mash.

**To preserve the color of cucumbers and remove bitterness, rub with salt and pickle for a short time** (5 to 6 hours in summer).

## Q21. Can I pickle a lot of vegetables at once?

**A21.** If you pickle too many vegetables at once, they may not ferment properly. Each ingredient needs to be surrounded with pickling mash, so **be sure to space them so they do not touch each other.**

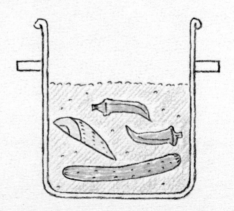

**Make sure vegetables are touching the pickling mash on all sides and are not crowded together in the bed.**

**Q23. Can I eat nukazuke pickles without rinsing off the pickling mash?**

**A23.** It is common to rinse off the pickling mash before eating, but **if the bed is healthy, you may eat the pickles without rinsing.** Alternately, simply wipe off the mash with your hands when you remove pickles from the bed.

**Q24. How long can I leave pickles in the bed?**

**A24.** Ginger, sansho pepper, kombu, garlic, and other antibacterial and **flavor-enhancing ingredients can be left in for a long time.** Three-year-old pickled garlic is very good. **Other vegetables, fish, and meats can become too salty or disintegrate if they are fermented too long, so take them out when they taste good to you.**

**Q25. How long do nukazuke pickles keep after they have been removed from the pickling bed?**

**A25. The secret to delicious nukazuke pickles is to eat them as soon as you remove them from the pickling bed.** Oxidation begins the moment the pickles comes into contact with air, damaging their color and flavor. If you can't eat them immediately, rinse the pickles, wrap them in plastic wrap and store in the refrigerator.

**Nukazuke pickles are best served immediately after removing from the pickling bed.**

## More About Nukazuke Pickles

**Q26. When removing pickles from the bed, is it safe to put the pickling mash clinging to the vegetables back in the bed?**

**A26. Yes. After removing pickles from the bed, scrape any mash that is stuck to them back into the pickling bed.** If you don't do this, the amount of mash will gradually decrease. Don't return the mash stuck to fish, meat, or other items pickled separately from the main bed.

**Q27. The surface of the pickling bed looks dark before I mix it. Is that OK?**

**A27.** The surface of the pickling bed will inevitably darken because it is exposed to air. This is because nuka is high in oil, which oxidizes in the presence of oxygen. **As long as the inside of the bed is a nice tan color, you have nothing to worry about.** After mixing the bed, flatten and smooth the surface to reduce the area exposed to oxygen.

**Q28. Are there any foods that I shouldn't put directly into the main pickling bed?**

**A28.** If fish and meat are pickled in the main bed, the vegetables you pickle will start to smell unpleasant. **Pickle fish and meat separately in ziplock bags.** Discard the mash that adheres to them.

    **Soft or fragile foods such as avocado and tofu should not be put in the main pickling bed.** Pickle them separately in a ziplock bag or similar container.

**Place ingredients like fish, meat and tofu in a ziplock bag and coat evenly with pickling mash.**

### Q29. What kinds of foods are not suitable for pickling?

**A29.** Most vegetables can be pickled, but **I do not recommend bitter or strong-smelling vegetables** such as bitter gourd, chicory, and leeks. **Ripe tomatoes, lettuce, and other vegetables with high water content should also be avoided.** Koyadofu, a nearly tasteless and odorless traditional freeze-dried tofu, does not taste good when pickled.

Hard vegetables such as burdock root, kabocha squash, bamboo shoots and potatoes should be boiled before pickling. Fish such as tuna, mackerel and sardines, as well as various meats, can also be pickled so long as they are kept separate from the main pickling bed.

### Q30. What can I add to the pickling bed to make it taste better?

**A30.** All you need to add are kombu for umami and chili peppers for their antiseptic properties. **The pickling bed will acquire a good flavor simply from adding fresh vegetables and mixing it every day.** Some people add beer or yogurt to promote fermentation, but I don't feel this is necessary. The lactobacilli in yogurt are difficult to propagate in a salty place like a nukazuke pickling bed, and beer may make the bed smell like alcohol. The naturally occurring lactobacilli in your bed will be sufficient. If you want to try tweaking the flavor, you can add dried sardines to increase umami, sansho pepper to enrich the flavor and provide antiseptic effects, or yuzu or tangerine peel to enhance the aroma (see p. 17 for more ideas).

When the pickling mash becomes low, add 1 scant cup (100 g) of new nuka for every 2 pounds (1 kg) of pickling bed, plus 7% of the new nuka's weight in salt.

Salt

New nuka

## Q31. The pickling bed is getting low. When should I add more nuka?

**A31.** The amount of pickling mash will gradually decrease as you remove vegetables with mash stuck to them or spill the mash when mixing. **If it looks low, add a cup or so of fresh nuka and 7% of the nuka's weight in salt (about 1 tsp).** Mix in the nuka and salt thoroughly and let the bed stand for 3 to 4 days undisturbed. When the smell of nuka disappears, you're ready to start pickling again. Avoid adding too much nuka at once, because it slows the fermentation process and changes the taste of the pickling bed.

## Q32. Does a pickling bed have an expiration date? When should it be discarded and remade from scratch?

**A32. A pickling bed is semi-permanent.** Some have been passed down from parent to child to grandchild for more than 100 years.

Don't be in a hurry to throw it away if it smells funny or loses its flavor. If you add new nuka and salt, the microorganisms will work to revive the bed. You don't need to throw it away or make a new batch unless it has been neglected for a long time and is covered with mold or has a bad smell that makes the pickles inedible. The longer you use your pickling bed to ferment vegetables, the more stable and deeply flavored it will become, and the less likely you will be to have problems. I encourage you to sustain your pickling at a slow, steady pace, as if you were raising a child or a pet.

**Q33. I've neglected my pickling bed for a long time. Can I use it again?**

**A33. A pickling bed that has been left untouched for a long time is likely to be unusable.** This is because microorganisms that cause putrid smells, such as butyric acid bacteria and film yeast, as well as various other bacteria will proliferate, and the bed is likely to become smelly. If you do not plan to pickle for a long time, store the pickling bed in the freezer.

**Q34. I received some mature pickling mash. Can I mix it with my own pickling bed that is already fermented?**

**A34.** If the pickling mash you receive is healthy, **you can mix it into to your own pickling bed.** The new mash may contribute different lactobacilli and yeasts, adding new flavors to your bed.

## Chapter 4

# Recipes Using Nukazuke Pickles and Nuka Pickling Mash

Nukazuke pickles are a real treat enjoyed straight out of the pickling bed.
But cooking with them brings their flavor and nutrients to a wide range of dishes,
livening up your repertoire with exciting new tastes. The pickling mash itself
can also be used as a seasoning, for instance in traditional recipes
where it is simmered with oily fish. I hope you'll use the recipes in this chapter
as a starting point for incorporating more nukazuke pickles into your daily diet!

# Basic Recipes for Soup Stock and Cooked Rice

## Dashi Soup Stock

**MAKES 1 QUART (1 LITER)**

¼ oz (10 g) dried kombu
1 quart (1 liter) water
½ oz (20 g) katsuobushi flakes
   (thinly shaved dried bonito)

**1.** Place the kombu and water in a medium pot and let sit at least 30 minutes, ideally overnight.
**2.** Heat over medium-low. Just before the water comes to a boil, remove the kombu.
**3.** Add the katsuobushi and simmer over low heat for 10 minutes. Remove from heat. When the katsuobushi sinks, strain broth through a fine strainer. Press gently to extract all the liquid.

## Vegetarian Dashi Soup Stock

**MAKES 1 QUART (1 LITER)**

¼ oz (10 g) dried kombu
1 quart (1 liter) water

**1.** Place the kombu and water in a jar with a lid and let sit overnight. Remove kombu before using the dashi.
**2.** Alternately, place the kombu and water in a pot and let sit at least 1 hour. Heat over medium-low. Just before the water comes to a boil, remove the kombu and turn off the heat.

## Steamed Rice

**MAKES ABOUT 2½ CUPS**

1 cup (200 g) short grain white rice
1 cup + 1 tablespoon (260 ml) water

**1.** In a strainer, thoroughly rinse the rice. Drain well and place in a medium saucepan with the water. Let sit 20 minutes.
**2.** Bring to a boil and reduce heat to low. Cover and cook for 8 minutes. Remove from heat and let sit with the lid on for 10 minutes to steam.

## Sushi Rice

**MAKES ABOUT 2½ CUPS**

1 recipe Steamed Rice
5 tablespoons rice vinegar
1 tablespoon + 1 teaspoon sugar
1¼ teaspoons salt

**1.** Prepare the Steamed Rice. While the rice is cooking, place the vinegar, sugar and salt in a small bowl and stir until the sugar and salt dissolve.
**2.** Transfer the cooked rice to a large, shallow wooden bowl. While still hot, pour the vinegar mixture evenly over it. Swiftly but gently fold the vinegar mixture into the rice with a wooden spatula. Cool the rice with a paper fan until it looks glossy. If not using immediately, cover with a damp towel to prevent the rice from drying out.

**Recipes Using Nukazuke Pickles** Nukazuke pickles can be used in many different recipes. Pickled ingredients are slightly salty and sour, with a deeper flavor than unpickled ones, so you'll be able to cook with less added salt than usual.

## Potato with Creamy Avocado

Rich pickled avocado is perfect for mashing and adding to sauces or dressings. Pair with simple steamed potatoes for an elegant side dish.

**SERVES 2**

½ Pickled Avocado (see page 44)
A pinch of salt
1 teaspoon olive oil
1 large boiling potato

**1.** Prepare the Pickled Avocado.
**2.** Rinse the pickling mash off the avocado and blot dry with paper towels. Place in a small bowl with the olive oil and mash with a fork until smooth, or use a mortar and pestle. Season to taste with salt.
**3.** Cut the potato into bite-size chunks and steam until tender. Transfer to the bowl of avocado and toss to coat, smashing the potatoes lightly as you mix.

# Sea Bream Carpaccio

Sushi-grade sea bream is fermented overnight in pickling mash and then thinly sliced for Japanese-style carpaccio. Despite its simplicity, the dish has a deep, umami-rich flavor. If you can't find sea bream (also called porgy), you may substitute sushi-grade red snapper or other white fish with a clean flavor.

**SERVES 3**

12 oz (350 g) Pickled Sea Bream
  (see recipe below)
¼ yellow onion
1 tablespoon capers, drained
1 tablespoon coarsely chopped
  Italian parsley
Salt and pepper to taste

**Carpaccio Sauce**
1 tablespoon soy sauce
½ tablespoon rice vinegar
½ tablespoon mirin
A pinch of salt
1 tablespoon olive oil

**1.** Prepare the Pickled Sea Bream as described below.

**2.** Thinly slice the onion from top to bottom. Soak the strips in a small bowl of cold water while you prepare the other ingredients. In a small bowl, whisk together the ingredients for the Carpaccio Sauce. Rinse the pickling mash off the sea bream and pat dry with paper towels. With a very sharp knife, slice the fish about ⅛ inch (3 mm) thick.

**3.** Drain the onion, pat dry, and divide between three serving plates. Arrange the sliced sea bream over the onion and pour the Carpaccio Sauce over the fish. Sprinkle with the capers and parsley and season to taste with salt and pepper.

▶ Pickled Sea Bream
Coat a piece of sushi-grade sea bream with pickling mash and place in a ziplock bag. Press out the air, seal, and pickle overnight.

# Pan-Fried Pork Chops

No seasoning needed! Just ferment pork chops overnight in pickling mash. The lactobacilli do the work of transforming the meat into a juicy, tender main dish full of umami.

**SERVES 2**

2 Pickled Pork Chops (see recipe below)
2 Japanese taro roots or boiling potatoes, about 2 oz (50 g) each
1 tablespoon sesame oil

**1.** Prepare the Pickled Pork Chops as described below.
**2.** Rinse the pickling mash off the pork chops and blot dry with paper towels. Steam the taro roots or potatoes until a wooden skewer can be easily inserted. Slice in half.
**3.** Heat the sesame oil in a skillet over medium-low, add the pork chops and taro root or potato, and cook until fragrant and browned, about 4 to 5 minutes per side. An instant-read thermometer inserted into the center of the pork chops should read 145°F (63°C).

▶ **Pickled Pork Chops**
Coat pork chops with pickling mash and place in a ziplock bag. Press out the air, seal, and pickle overnight.

## Sautéed Chicken with Leeks

Pickling makes chicken deliciously tender and mild. No seasoning is needed beyond the savory leeks.

**SERVES 2**

2 boneless Pickled Chicken
    Thighs, about ¼ lb (115 g)
    each (page 41)
2 small leeks or fat green onions
1 tablespoon sesame oil

**1.** Prepare the Pickled Chicken Thighs.
**2.** Rinse the pickling mash off the chicken thighs and blot dry with paper towels. Cut into 1 inch (2.5 cm) cubes. Thickly slice the leeks or green onions.
**3.** Heat the sesame oil in a skillet over medium-low. Add the chicken, skin side down. When browned, flip and fry the other side a few more minutes, until cooked through.
**4.** Add the leek or green onion and sauté until softened and browned.

## Crispy Squid Balls

Made without any fillers, these squid balls are surprisingly satisfying and full of umami. Squid tends to splatter when deep-fried, but pickling removes excess moisture, so there's less need to worry about flying hot oil when making this recipe.

**MAKES ABOUT 10 MEDIUM BALLS**

1 medium Pickled Squid, about
   12 oz (350 g) (page 40)
1 piece green onion, about
   4 inches (10 cm)
A knob of ginger, peeled
Cornstarch or potato starch for
   dusting
Oil for deep-frying
Green beans for garnish (optional)

1. Prepare the Pickled Squid.
2. Finely chop the green onion and ginger. Rinse the pickling mash off the squid and blot dry. Process to a paste in a food processor.
3. Add the green onion and ginger to the squid paste and pulse briefly to combine. Lightly moisten your hands and form the paste into 10 balls.
4. Dust the squid balls lightly with cornstarch or potato starch. Let rest for 10 to 15 minutes. Meanwhile, in a wok or deep skillet, heat several inches (about 8 cm) of oil to 340°F (170°C). Fry the balls until golden brown, remove with a slotted spoon, and drain on paper towels. Optionally garnish with blanched green beans.

## Pickled Tofu and Vegetable Salad (Shira-Ae)

Shira-ae is a classic Japanese side dish of seasoned mashed tofu studded with vegetables. Here the dish gets a complete update with savory, slightly sour pickled tofu. The vegetables are also pickled, lending even greater depth to the flavor. Serve small portions alongside steamed rice and other accompaniments.

**SERVES 2**

¼ block Pickled Tofu, about 3 oz (85g) (page 51)
1 piece Pickled Carrot, about 1¼ in (3 cm) long (page 33)
2 pieces Pickled Komatsuna Greens (page 29) or other pickled greens
½ teaspoon mirin
A pinch of salt

**1.** Prepare the Pickled Tofu, Pickled Carrot, and Pickled Komatsuna Greens.
**2.** Mash the tofu in a mortar and pestle or food processor. Add the mirin and salt to taste.
**3.** Cut the carrot in thin matchsticks. Chop the greens in 1 inch (2.5 cm) lengths.
**4.** Add the chopped vegetables to the mashed tofu and mix well.

## Chicken Tender and Kombu Soup

Because the chicken tenders and kombu are fermented overnight, this soup has amazing umami without adding stock or seasonings. The portions given here make a small side dish to serve with a Japanese-style meal.

**SERVES 2**

1 Pickled Chicken Tender, about 2 oz (55 g) (see recipe below)
4 in (10 cm) piece Pickled Kombu (page 49)
A small knob of ginger
2 in (5 cm) piece green onion
1 teaspoon sesame oil
½ teaspoon toasted sesame seeds
1¼ cups (300 ml) water

**1.** Prepare the Pickled Chicken Tender as described below, and the Pickled Kombu.
**2.** Rinse the pickling mash off the chicken tender, blot dry with paper towels, and cut into bite-size pieces. Rinse the pickling mash off the kombu, blot dry with paper towels, and thinly slice. Shred the ginger and cut the green onion into thin diagonal slices.
**3.** Heat the sesame oil in a small pot over medium-low and sauté the ginger, green onion and kombu. When fragrant, add the chicken and water and simmer for about 10 minutes. Divide between two bowls and sprinkle with the toasted sesame seeds.

▶ Pickled Chicken Tender
Coat chicken tender with pickling mash and place in a ziplock bag. Press out the air, seal and pickle overnight.

# Beef, Bell Pepper and Bamboo Shoot Stir-Fry

Pickled bamboo shoots have a robust flavor, as if they are already seasoned. Nukazuke turns even this everyday Chinese-style staple into a refreshingly tangy new dish.

**SERVES 2**

2 oz (60 g) Pickled Bamboo Shoot
  (page 36)
2 small green bell peppers
3 oz (85 g) thinly sliced beef sirloin
1 knob ginger, peeled
1 green onion
1 teaspoon cooking sake
1 teaspoon soy sauce
½ tablespoon cornstarch or potato starch
1 tablespoon sesame oil

**Sauce**
½ clove garlic, grated
2 tablespoons cooking sake
1½ tablespoons soy sauce
1 tablespoon mirin
1 teaspoon miso (preferably soybean miso)

**1.** Prepare the Pickled Bamboo Shoot.
**2.** Rinse the pickling mash off the bamboo shoot, pat dry with paper towels, and slice thinly. Remove the stem and seeds from the bell peppers and slice thinly. Thinly slice the beef. Finely chop the ginger and green onion.
**3.** Season the beef with 1 teaspoon each of soy sauce and sake and sprinkle with cornstarch or potato starch. The starch locks in the meat's juices to keep it moist, and gives it a creamy finish.
**4.** Combine the sauce ingredients in a small bowl. Heat the sesame oil in a skillet over medium-low, add the green onion, ginger and beef, and stir-fry until the beef is cooked through. Add the bamboo shoot and green peppers and stir-fry until wilted.
**5.** Add the sauce ingredients and stir-fry for another minute or two.

# Egg Tartar Sauce

Richly flavored pickled egg makes a great topping all by itself, simply chopped or mashed. Mixing in pickled cucumber adds complexity and a hint of sourness. Serve with deep-fried foods such as breaded scallops.

**SERVES 2**

1 Pickled Egg (page 50)
½ small Pickled Cucumber
  (page 28)
¼ small onion
A pinch of salt
1 teaspoon rice vinegar
1 tablespoon olive oil

**1.** Prepare the Pickled Egg and Pickled Cucumber.
**2.** Rinse the pickling mash off the egg and cucumber and blot dry with paper towels. Chop finely. Finely mince the onion.
**3.** Place the chopped pickles and onion in a medium bowl with the salt, vinegar and olive oil, and mix well.

# Horse Mackerel and Persimmon Spring Rolls

Pickling concentrates the umami of horse mackerel (*aji*) and does away with its strong odor. Make sure to use firm Fuyu persimmons rather than Hachiya persimmons, which are too soft for this recipe when ripe. Other oily fish such as sardines can be substituted.

**SERVES 2**

2 medium Pickled Horse Mackerel
  fillets, about 3 oz (85 g) (see
  recipe below)
¼ Fuyu persimmon
2 spring roll wrappers
A pinch of salt
A dash of soy sauce
Cornstarch or potato starch
Oil for deep-frying

**1.** Prepare the Pickled Horse Mackerel as described below.
**2.** Rinse the pickling mash off the fish, blot with paper towels, and chop until you have a sticky paste. Cut the persimmon into ⅓ inch (1 cm) cubes, leaving the peel on. Cut the spring roll wrappers in half.
**3.** In a small bowl, stir together the horse mackerel, salt, soy sauce and persimmon. Divide the filling in four, spoon along the wrappers, and roll up, securing the ends with moistened cornstarch or potato starch. In a wok or deep skillet, heat several inches (about 8 cm) of oil to 340°F (170°C). Fry the spring rolls until golden, remove with a slotted spoon, and drain on paper towels.

▶ Pickled Horse Mackerel
Fillet the fish, remove remaining bones, sprinkle with salt and let sit for about an hour. Blot off the moisture and coat with pickling mash. Place in a ziplock bag, seal, and pickle overnight.

## Penne with Nukazuke Mushrooms

Cheese and nukazuke pickles are a glorious fermented-food pairing. Using several kinds of mushrooms deepens the umami and gives the dish a rich, full flavor.

**SERVES 2**

5 oz (150 g) mixed Pickled Mushrooms such as king oyster, shiitake and button (page 45)
4 oz (120 g) dried penne
1 clove garlic
1 tablespoon olive oil
1 tablespoon soy milk
Parmesan cheese to taste
Salt and pepper to taste
Soy sauce to taste
1 tablespoon minced parsley

**1.** Prepare the Pickled Mushrooms.
**2.** Cook the penne until al dente in plenty of boiling salted water.
**3.** Rinse the pickling mash from the mushrooms, pat dry with paper towels, and cut into bite-size pieces. Finely mince the garlic.
**4.** Heat the olive oil over low heat in a skillet. Add the garlic and sauté until fragrant. Add the mushrooms and sauté until softened, then stir in the penne, soy milk and grated Parmesan. Remove from heat and season with salt, pepper and soy sauce. Divide between two serving dishes and top with minced parsley and more Parmesan.

## Apple and Napa Cabbage Salad

Even a simple salad gains complex umami from the addition of apples fermented overnight in the pickling bed. The result is an elegant side dish with a difference.

**SERVES 2**

⅓ Pickled Apple (page 48)
2 leaves napa cabbage
Salt
A small knob of ginger
2½ in (5 cm) piece kombu
½ yuzu or lemon

**1.** Prepare the Pickled Apple.
**2.** Cut the cabbage into bite-size pieces, sprinkle with salt, and set aside while you prepare the other ingredients.
**3.** Rinse the pickling mash off the apple and blot dry with paper towels. Cut lengthwise into several pieces and slice crosswise thinly. Finely shred the ginger. Wrap the kombu in a wet cloth and let sit until softened, then use kitchen scissors to cut into thin strips. Zest and juice the yuzu or lemon.
**4.** Squeeze the cabbage pieces to remove excess moisture. In a medium bowl, toss with the apple, ginger and kombu. Add the yuzu juice and zest and mix well.

**Recipes Using Old Nukazuke Pickles**
Long-fermented or "old" nukazuke pickles have a powerfully sour, salty flavor all their own. The length of time required to make this type of pickle varies depending on what you're pickling, the season, and the location of your pickling bed. For example, cucumbers take two days in summer while daikon radishes can take four days or more in winter. Take advantage of the punch these "old pickles" pack in your cooking.

# Refreshing Udon with Chopped Vegetables

In Japanese, "dashi" usually means stock, but in Yamagata Prefecture, it also means a mixture of finely chopped vegetables like the one topping these noodles. Cold udon topped with "dashi" makes a great summer meal, and with old pickles it's even more refreshing and nutritious. For the soup stock, either make your own or use instant dashi powder from an Asian grocery store.

**SERVES 2**

½ old Pickled Cucumber (page 28)
½ old Pickled Salad Turnip
   (page 27)
1 old Pickled Myoga (Japanese
   Ginger) (page 37) or knob
   of ginger
½ old Pickled Eggplant (page 32)
1 cup (250 ml) Dashi Soup Stock
   (page 74), cooled
½ tablespoon soy sauce
½ tablespoon mirin
2 oz (55 g) dry udon noodles

**1.** Prepare the Pickled Cucumber, Pickled Salad Turnip, Pickled Myoga if using, Pickled Eggplant, and Dashi Soup Stock.
**2.** Rinse the pickling mash off the cucumber, turnip, myoga and eggplant. Blot dry with paper towels and chop the cucumber, turnip, and eggplant roughly into ¼ inch (5 mm) dice. Shred the myoga or ginger. Place in a medium bowl with the stock, soy sauce and mirin and mix well.
**3.** Boil the udon noodles in unsalted water until al dente, 8 to 10 minutes. Drain and rinse well under running water, rubbing between your hands to remove excess starch. Drain well.
**4.** Divide the noodles between two shallow bowls and top with the pickle mixture.

▶ See below for how to make old pickles.

## How to Make Old Nukazuke Pickles

To make old nukazuke pickles, add 12 hours to the pickling times given in the instructions in summer and a day or more in winter. This will allow ingredients to fully ferment. Monitor the flavor by tasting periodically and remove when it tastes strong enough to you.

▶ **Old Pickled Shungiku (Garland Chrysanthemum)**
Rub the shungiku with salt, squeeze thoroughly to remove excess moisture, and pickle for 1 day.

▶ **Old Pickled Atsuage (Thick Deep-Fried Tofu)** Coat the tofu with pickling mash and place in a ziplock bag. Seal and pickle for at least 2 days.

## Soybean and Pickled Ginger Tempura

Fried food can be heavy, but incorporating pickles lends a refreshing aftertaste. This recipe calls for red pickled ginger (*beni shoga*), which is isn't sweet like the pink pickled ginger (*gari*) served with sushi. It is available at Japanese grocery stores. The intense flavor of old pickled soybeans goes well with the sourness of the ginger.

**SERVES 2**

1 scant cup (140 g) old Pickled
   Soybeans (page 50)
½ oz (20 g) red pickled ginger
1 tablespoon flour

**For the batter**
4 tablespoons cake flour
5 to 6 tablespoons water

Oil for deep-frying

**1.** Prepare the old Pickled Soybeans.
**2.** Rinse the pickling mash off the soybeans and pat dry with paper towels. In a medium bowl, combine with the pickled ginger. Dust with 1 tablespoon of flour and toss.
**3.** Place the batter ingredients in a small bowl and mix with a few swift strokes of a fork or chopsticks. Stir the soybeans and ginger into the batter.
**4.** In a wok or deep skillet, heat a few inches (about 8 cm) of oil to 340°F (170°C). Drop spoonfuls of batter into the oil and fry until golden. Remove with a slotted spoon and drain on paper towels.

▶ See page 91 for how to make old pickles.

# Futomaki Sushi

Intensely flavored old pickles work wonderfully in sushi. There is no need to cook the vegetables after pickling, making this recipe quick and convenient. Futomaki are fat sushi rolls with several fillings. You can also use one pickled ingredient at a time for thin rolls (hosomaki), or mix pickled and unpickled ingredients.

**SERVES 2**

8 in (20 cm) piece old Pickled Carrot (page 33)

8 in (20 cm) piece old Pickled Burdock Root (page 29)

8 in (20 cm) piece old Pickled Cucumber (page 28)

4 oz (100 g) old Pickled Tuna (page 39)

2 scant cups (300 g) prepared Sushi Rice (page 74)

2 sheets nori seaweed

**1.** Prepare the old Pickled Carrot, Pickled Burdock Root, Pickled Cucumber and Pickled Tuna. Prepare the Sushi Rice.
**2.** Rinse the pickling mash off the vegetables and fish and blot dry with paper towels. Cut the vegetables lengthwise into ¼ inch strips about the same length as the nori. Cut the tuna in similar strips.
**3.** Divide the rice evenly between the two sheets of nori. Place half the tuna and one strip of each vegetable in the center of each roll (you will have extra; if the vegetables are too short, combine several pieces.) Moisten a sharp knife with a wet dish towel and slice the sushi roll.

▶ See page 91 for how to make old pickles.

## Chilled Horse Mackerel and Rice Soup

Use fish that has fermented for at least 24 hours for this dish. It is salty and packed with umami, providing plenty of flavor simply pounded and thinned with stock. If you can't find horse mackerel (*aji*), substitute other types of mackerel or oily fish such as sardines or herring.

**SERVES 2**

2 medium old Pickled Horse
  Mackerel fillets, about 3 oz
  (85 g) (see recipe below)
1 small cucumber
Salt
4 green shiso leaves
A knob of ginger, peeled
1 teaspoon roasted sesame
  seeds
1 cup Steamed Rice (page 74)
1 cup (250 ml) or more Dashi
  Soup Stock (page 74)
A dash of soy sauce

**1.** Prepare the Pickled Horse Mackerel as described below. Prepare the Dashi Soup Stock.
**2.** Thinly slice the cucumber, massage with salt and drain. Shred the shiso and ginger. Rinse the pickling mash off the horse mackerel, blot dry with paper towels, and grill until cooked through. Remove any bones, shred, and grind in a mortar and pestle or food processor. Transfer to a medium bowl.
**3.** Thin the fish paste to taste with the stock. Add the cucumber and sesame seeds and season with soy sauce if needed. Chill in the refrigerator. When ready to serve, divide the rice between two bowls, pour the soup over it, and top with shiso and ginger.

---

▶ **Old Pickled Horse Mackerel**
Fillet the fish, sprinkle with salt and let sit for about an hour. Blot off the moisture and coat with pickling mash. Place in a ziplock bag, seal, and pickle for at least 24 hours.

---

# Tricolor Korean-Style Salad

The key to this version of the Korean side dish called *namul* is the fragrance of the heated sesame oil, which mellows the pungency of the pickles. Substitute other types of mushrooms and greens if shiitake and shungiku (garland chrysanthemum) are not available.

**SERVES 2**

1½ in (4 cm) piece old Pickled
  Carrot (page 33)
2 old Pickled Shiitake
  Mushrooms (page 45)
3 to 4 pieces old Pickled
  Shungiku (page 91)

**A Ingredients**
½ teaspoon grated ginger
1 teaspoon roasted white
  sesame seeds
1 teaspoon sesame oil

**B Ingredients**
1 garlic clove, grated
1 teaspoon roasted white
  sesame seeds
1 teaspoon sesame oil

**C Ingredients**
½ teaspoon grated ginger
1 teaspoon roasted black
  sesame seeds
1 teaspoon sesame oil

**1.** Prepare the Pickled Carrot, Pickled Mushrooms, and Pickled Shungiku.
**2.** Rinse the pickling mash off the vegetables and pat dry with paper towels. Cut the carrot into thin strips. Cut the stems and caps of the mushrooms into thin strips. Cut the greens into 1½ inch (4 cm) pieces. Place each vegetable in a separate small bowl.
**3.** Heat 3 teaspoons of sesame oil for the A, B and C dressings.
**4.** Add the A ingredients to the bowl of carrots and mix. Add the B ingredients to the bowl of mushrooms and mix. Add the C ingredients to the bowl of greens and mix. Divide the vegetables between two serving dishes.

# Spicy and Sour Vegetable Hot Pot

The combination of three types of sour food—old pickled vegetables, tomatoes and black vinegar—adds complexity to the flavor. The acidity balances the spiciness of the chili oil.

**SERVES 2**

2½ in (5 cm) piece old **Pickled Carrot (page 33)**
1 old **Pickled Shiitake Mushroom (page 45)**
2 oz (50 g) old **Pickled Bamboo Shoot (page 36)**
1 **tomato**
⅓ **block firm tofu, about 4 oz (100 g)**
1 **dried wood ear mushroom**
2½ in (5 cm) piece **green onion**
1 **egg**
1⅔ cups (400 ml) **water**
1 tablespoon **cooking sake**
1 teaspoon **soy sauce**
½ tablespoon **corn or potato starch**
1 teaspoon **Chinese black vinegar**
**Salt and pepper to taste**
**Chili oil to taste**
**Fresh coriander to taste, chopped**

**1.** Prepare the old Pickled Carrot, Pickled Shiitake Mushroom, and Pickled Bamboo Shoot.
**2.** Rinse the pickling mash off the vegetables, pat dry with paper towels and slice thinly. Roughly chop the tomato. Cut the tofu into bite-size cubes. Soak the wood ear mushroom in water until rehydrated and slice thinly. Cut the green onion into thin diagonal slices.
**3.** Put the water and the pickled vegetables into a medium saucepan or clay pot and bring to a simmer over medium-low heat. Add the tofu, tomato, wood ear mushroom and green onion and simmer for 3 to 4 minutes. Add the sake and soy sauce.
**4.** Dissolve the corn or potato starch in ½ tablespoon water. Stir into the soup and simmer briefly to thicken. Add the beaten egg, turn off the heat and stir. Add the black vinegar and salt to taste. Offer the black pepper, chili oil and coriander at the table.

▶ See page 91 for how to make old pickles.

# Mushroom Pâté

This rich, full-bodied pâté will have your guests guessing what the secret ingredient is. You can use any kind of mushrooms, but combining several kinds will deepen the flavor. Serve with slices of baguette or vegetable sticks.

**SERVES 2**

5 oz (150 g) mixed old Pickled
  Mushrooms (page 45)
½ small onion
2 tablespoon canola oil, divided
½ tablespoon miso
Salt and black pepper to taste

1. Prepare the Pickled Mushrooms.
2. Finely mince the onion. Rinse the pickling mash off the old pickled mushrooms and pat dry with paper towels.
3. Heat 1 tablespoon of the oil in a skillet over medium-low and stir-fry the onions and mushrooms until wilted.
4. Transfer the mushrooms and onions to a food processor, add the miso and remaining oil, and process until smooth. Season to taste with salt and pepper.

▶ See page 91 for how to make old pickles.

## Fried Nukazuke Potatoes

Old pickled potatoes make surprisingly delicious French fries. They taste like sour cream.

**SERVES 2**

1 large old Pickled Potato (page 31)
1 tablespoon cornstarch or potato starch
Black pepper to taste
1 teaspoon fresh thyme
Oil for deep-frying

**1.** Prepare the Pickled Potato.
**2.** Rinse the pickling mash off the potato, pat dry with paper towels, and cut into wedges with the skin on. Mince the thyme.
**3.** Sprinkle the potato wedges with the cornstarch or potato starch and half the thyme. Heat 1 to 2 inches (about 5 cm) of oil in a wok or deep skillet to 350°F (175°C). Fry the potatoes until they are pale golden, about 5 minutes.
**4.** Arrange on a serving dish and sprinkle with black pepper and the remaining thyme.

▶ See page 91 for how to make old pickles.

## Tofu Caprese

Old pickled tofu tastes like cheese, and layering it with fruit makes an unusual variation on caprese salad. Make sure to use Fuyu rather than Hachiya persimmons, which are too soft for this recipe when ripe. Figs, peaches and pears are tasty alternatives.

**SERVES 2**

¼ block old Pickled Tofu (silken), about 3 oz (85 g)
1 ripe Fuyu persimmon
½ tablespoon olive oil
Salt and pepper to taste
3 leaves fresh basil
Honey to taste

**1.** Prepare the old Pickled Tofu.
**2.** Slice the tofu ¼ inch (7 mm) wide. Peel and slice the persimmon to a similar thickness. Tear the basil leaves into small pieces
**3.** On a serving plate, arrange the tofu and persimmon in alternating layers. Drizzle with the olive oil and season to taste with salt, black pepper and honey. Scatter with the basil.

▶ See page 91 for how to make old pickles.

## Stir-Fried Summer Vegetables and Pork with Miso

Tangy old pickled vegetables taste incredible with rich soybean miso. Doubanjiang, a spicy Chinese bean paste available at Asian grocery stores, gives the dish a bit of spice.

**SERVES 2**

1 small old Pickled Eggplant (page 32)
2 old Pickled Bell Peppers (page 33), one red and one yellow
4 oz (100 g) pork belly
1 garlic clove
1 tablespoon sesame oil

**Sauce**
1 tablespoon soybean or other miso
½ tablespoon cooking sake
1 tablespoon mirin
½ teaspoon doubanjiang
Sesame oil

1. Prepare the Pickled Eggplant and Pickled Bell Peppers.
2. Rinse the pickling mash off the eggplant and bell peppers and pat dry with paper towels. Cut into bite-size pieces. Thinly slice the pork belly. Mince the garlic. Whisk the sauce ingredients in a small bowl.
3. Heat the sesame oil in a skillet over medium-low. Stir-fry the garlic and pork until the pork is cooked through. Add the pickled vegetables and stir-fry another 2 to 3 minutes.
4. Add the sauce and cook an additional 1 to 2 minutes.

▶ See page 91 for how to make old pickles.

# Nukazuke Fried Rice

If the old pickles are well flavored, fried rice does not need additional seasoning. If they have only been pickled for a short time, season the fried rice to taste with salt or soy sauce. Fried rice is an accommodating dish—if komatsuna greens or burdock are not available, substitute other pickled vegetables such as mushrooms, celery, or bell pepper. Day-old rice works well in this recipe.

**SERVES 2**

3 to 4 pieces old Pickled
  Komatsuna Greens (page 29)
4 in (10 cm) piece old Pickled
  Burdock Root (page 29)
1 in (3 cm) piece of carrot
1 garlic clove
1 egg
1 tablespoon sesame oil
1½ cups (300 g) cooked rice (page
  74)

**1.** Prepare the old Pickled Komatsuna Greens and Pickled Burdock Root.
**2.** Rinse the pickling mash off the greens and burdock root, pat dry with paper towels, and chop finely. Mince the carrot and garlic clove. In a small bowl, beat the egg.
**3.** Heat a wok over medium-low and add half the sesame oil. Add the egg and mix quickly. When it is fluffy and set, remove to a plate.
**4.** Add the remaining sesame oil to the same wok. Add the garlic, carrot and old pickles in that order and stir-fry until well cooked. Add the rice and stir-fry for 1 to 2 minutes. Add the cooked egg, mix in, and serve immediately.

▶ See page 91 for how to make old pickles.

## Thai-Style Stir-Fried Noodles

The complex flavor of pickled deep-fried tofu pairs well with the Thai-style ingredients in this recipe. Add fish sauce at the table for an extra flavor kick.

**SERVES 2**

1 block of old Pickled Atsuage (thick deep-fried tofu) (page 91), about 5 oz (150 g)
5 oz (150 g) Thai cellophane noodles
5 garlic chives or green onions
2 oz (50 g) bean sprouts
1 egg
2 tablespoons sesame oil
⅓ oz (10 g) small dried shrimp
1 tablespoon water
Salt and soy sauce to taste
Roasted chopped peanuts to taste
¼ lemon, cut in wedges

**1.** Prepare the Pickled Atsuage.

**2.** Rinse the pickling mash off the tofu, pat dry with paper towels and cut into 1 inch (2 cm) dice. Soak the cellophane noodles in plenty of boiling water for about 10 minutes and drain in a colander. Roughly slice the garlic chives or green onions. Blanch and drain the bean sprouts. Beat the egg well.

**3.** Heat a wok over medium-low and add half the sesame oil. Add the egg and mix quickly. When it is fluffy and set, remove to a plate.

**4.** Add the remaining sesame oil to the same wok, add the dried shrimp and stir-fry until fragrant. Add the noodles and water and stir-fry, separating the noodles with a pair of cooking chopsticks or spoon.

**5.** When the noodles are semi-transparent, add the fried tofu, cooked egg, bean sprouts and garlic chives or green onions and stir-fry briefly. Season with salt and soy sauce and arrange on serving plates. Scatter with the peanuts and garnish with lemon wedges.

**Recipes Using Nuka Pickling Mash**
Adding pickling mash to recipes increases both umami and nutritional value. Because it is moist, the mash works especially well in simmered recipes. Only use mash from a bed that is healthy and free of unpleasant odors.

# Mackerel Simmered with Pickling Mash

In this dish from Kitakyushu in southern Japan, the pickling mash counteracts mackerel's fishy odor and tenderizes the fish. The rich flavor is addictive!

**SERVES 2**

1 mackerel fillet, about 8 oz (225 g)
A knob of ginger, peeled
½ cup (100 ml) water
1 tablespoon soy sauce
1 tablespoon mirin
1 tablespoon cooking sake
2 tablespoons pickling mash

**1.** Cut the mackerel fillet in half. Finely shred the ginger.
**2.** Put the water, soy sauce, mirin and sake in a medium saucepan or clay pot and bring to a simmer over medium-low heat. Add the mackerel and ginger and simmer for about 10 minutes.
**3.** Add the pickling mash and simmer over low heat for 2 to 3 minutes. It is ready when the mash has dissolved into the liquid.

To preserve the flavor of nuka, first cook the mackerel in broth and then add the pickling mash. Be careful not to let the mash burn after you add it.

# Pork Simmered with Pickling Mash and Sansho Pepper

Pork is marinated with seasoned pickling mash, then cooked in the marinade. After fermenting in pickling mash and miso, the pork is incredibly tender, even with a short cooking time. Sichuan pepper may be substituted for the sansho pepper; they are similarly fragrant relatives.

**SERVES 3**

10 oz (300 g) block of fatty pork, such as shoulder or belly
2 oz (50 g) pickling mash
2 oz (50 g) miso
3 tablespoons + 1 teaspoon cooking sake
1 tablespoon + 2 teaspoons mirin
A knob of ginger, peeled
2½ cups (600 ml) water
About 10 sansho peppercorns, fresh, dried or powdered.
  For powder, use about ½ teaspoon.

**1.** Put the pork in a ziplock bag with the pickling mash, miso, sake and mirin. Marinate overnight in the refrigerator. Shred the ginger.
**2.** Put the pork and marinade in a medium pot. Add the water, ginger and sansho pepper and heat over medium-low. When it comes to a boil, reduce the heat to low and simmer gently for 40 to 50 minutes, until a wooden skewer pierces the meat easily.

The pork is marinated overnight in a ziplock bag, then simmered with the marinade.

### Recipes Using Nuka

Both raw and toasted nuka can be used in savory and sweet dishes. The faint sweetness of raw nuka is reminiscent of *kinako*, a roasted soybean powder popular in Japanese sweets. Nuka from organic rice is best for these recipes. For toasted nuka, either purchase *irinuka*, which is already toasted, or toast your own in a skillet over low heat for 2 to 3 minutes.

# Creamy Root Vegetable Gratin

Used as a topping in baked dishes, raw nuka tastes a bit like grated cheese. Sake lees are worth searching for at a Japanese grocery store or sake brewery. They add richness and umami to the gratin, and whatever you don't use here can be added to Japanese recipes like pickles and hotpots.

**SERVES 2**

1 large salad turnip
2 taro roots, about 2 oz (50 g) each
2 teaspoons olive oil
A pinch of salt
¾ cup (200 ml) unsweetened soy milk
1 tablespoon sake lees
1½ tablespoons cornstarch or potato starch
½ teaspoon salt
2 tablespoons (10 g) raw nuka

**1.** Cut the turnip into about 12 wedges, leaving the skin on. Steam the taro roots until a wooden skewer pierces them easily, peel and cut into bite-size pieces.
**2.** Heat the olive oil in a skillet over medium-low and add the turnips and salt. Sauté until browned.
**3.** To make the sauce, combine the soy milk, sake lees, cornstarch or potato starch and ½ teaspoon of salt in a small saucepan and mix well to dissolve the starch and sake lees. Heat over low, stirring constantly, until the liquid is thickened.
**4.** Arrange the turnip and taro root in an oven-proof dish, pour the sauce over them, and sprinkle the raw nuka on top. Broil until the top is browned, watching carefully to make sure it doesn't burn.

# Hamburger Steaks with Toasted Nuka

The toasted nuka in this recipe stands in for breadcrumbs. Its sweetness and texture make for deliciously light hamburger steaks.

**SERVES 2**

¼ onion
1 tablespoon plus 1 teaspoon olive oil
About 2 oz (50 g) maitake or other mushrooms
2½ oz (75 g) ground beef
2½ oz (75 g) ground pork
3 tablespoons (15 g) toasted nuka
Salt and pepper to taste
1 cup broccoli florets, steamed

**Sauce**
1 tablespoon balsamic vinegar
1 tablespoon soy sauce
1 tablespoon mirin

**1.** Mince the onion. Heat 1 teaspoon of the olive oil in a small skillet over medium-low and sauté the onion. Trim the tough ends off the maitake mushrooms and pull apart into small clusters. If using other mushrooms, trim and cut into bite-size pieces. In a small saucepan, whisk together the Sauce ingredients.
**2.** In a medium bowl, thoroughly combine the ground beef, ground pork, sautéed onion, toasted nuka, and salt and pepper. Form into two oval patties.
**3.** Heat the remaining olive oil in a skillet over medium-low and brown the hamburger patties on one side. Tuck the maitake mushrooms around the patties. Flip the patties and brown the other side.
**4.** Cook the Sauce over medium-low until thickened.
**5.** Arrange the hamburger steaks, mushrooms and steamed broccoli on two serving plates and pour the Sauce over the meat.

# Toasted Nuka Cookies

The flavor of toasted nuka shines in these simple cookies. Since nuka is naturally sweet, not much additional sweetener is needed. Substitute maple syrup for the honey to make them vegan.

**MAKES 25 SMALL COOKIES**

2 tablespoons (10 g) toasted nuka
1 cup (100 g) cake flour
½ teaspoon aluminum-free baking powder
A pinch of salt
1½ tablespoons honey
2 tablespoons canola oil

**1.** Combine the toasted nuka, cake flour, baking powder and salt in a medium bowl and mix well with a whisk.
**2.** Put the canola oil and honey in a separate bowl and whisk together. Stir the wet ingredients into the dry ingredients until well combined.
**3.** Cover the bowl and chill in the refrigerator for 30 minutes. On a floured surface, roll to a thickness of about ⅕ inch (5 mm) and cut out with cookie cutters. Re-roll the scraps to make more cookies. Transfer cookies to a non-stick cookie sheet.
**4.** Bake the cookies in a preheated 350°F (180°C) oven for about 10 minutes, until lightly browned on the bottom. Remove from the oven and cool on the sheet before transferring to a plate.

# Castella Cake

A Castella cake is a simple type of sponge cake. This version is cooked in a skillet, which gives it a rather rustic appearance. The key is to cook it slowly over low heat to brown it evenly.

**SERVES 2**

2 tablespoons raw nuka
¾ cup plus 2 teaspoons (80 g) cake flour
2 eggs
2½ tablespoons sugar
1 tablespoon honey
1 teaspoon canola oil

**1.** Separate the eggs. In a medium bowl, thoroughly whisk the egg yolks and sugar together. Add the honey and whisk to incorporate.
**2.** In a separate bowl, using a clean whisk, whip the egg whites until soft peaks form. With a rubber spatula, fold into the yolk mixture.
**3.** Sift the raw nuka and cake flour into a small bowl and fold gently into the wet ingredients.
**4.** Rub a medium skillet with the oil, pour in the batter and cover tightly with aluminum foil. Cook over low heat for 10 to 15 minutes. Flip and cook on the other side for about 5 minutes. The cake is done when a wooden skewer inserted into the center comes out clean.

---

**NOTE: This cake burns easily. Removing the skillet from the burner and placing it on a wet cloth several times while cooking to cool the pan will help prevent burning.**

---

# My Fermentation Lifestyle

In my household, we make many fermented and pickled foods in addition to nukazuke—miso, natto, pickled plums, shibazuke pickles tinted purple with shiso leaves, salt-fermented napa cabbage, daikon radish pickles aged in salted nuka or marinated in sweet amazake, and more. Each season has its own pickles. Many pickling ingredients are in season only for a very short time, like the ume (Japanese apricots) used in pickled plums. The seasons do not wait for us, so we are always scrambling to capture their delicious flavors.

But strangely enough, even with the pressures of work, chores, and childcare, I have never once thought, "Well, I guess I won't pickle this year." Washing dozens of daikon radishes in cold water, silently poking holes in ume with a bamboo skewer, and diligently crushing soybeans... I love each and every one of these tasks and feel proud to do them. I love the time I spend in the presence of fruits and vegetables, with a quiet, still mind. The resulting

**"Dai's umeboshi" are pickled plums that I made from fruit I gathered in the garden the year my son Dai was born. I pickled 100 of them, hoping that he would eat one on his birthday every year until he turned 100 years old.**

pickles are seasonal gifts that warm the hearts and bodies of family and friends. Whenever I feel that I have eaten a little too much at a restaurant or my stomach is upset, my medicine is nukazuke pickles, natto, and miso soup. They never fail to sooth my digestive system.

The practice of preparing seasonal fermented foods was passed down from my grandmother and mother to me, and now I am passing it down to my son Dai. At the age of two, Dai already has his own little nukazuke pickling bed. Although he spills the bran everywhere, he diligently pickles his favorite vegetables. If he's not in the mood to mix his bed, I have one more job to do, but my wish is that he will keep his pickling bed for decades. I hope it will go with him when he starts his own family, and that he will always feel close to fermented foods and the microorganisms that create them.

The flavor of fermented foods varies from person to person. Even if my students all use the same ingredients in a nukazuke pickling class, the taste of their pickles always varies slightly. That's the interesting thing about fermented foods: the particular microorganisms on our hands, in our homes, and on the vegetables we use create the unique taste of our food—our family flavor, you might say. Nukazuke pickles in particular are likely to be inhabited by the bacteria living around you because you mix the bed by hand every day. It is are ideally suited to you, and will help you and your family become healthier at the same time that it gives you the pickles that taste the most delicious to you.

This chapter was written with the assistance of Shigeo Miyao, Doctor of Agriculture (Professor, Tokyo Kasei University; Visiting Professor, Sichuan University; Vice President, Japan Traditional Foods Research Association; Senior Advisor, Japan Federation of Pickle Cooperatives).

**Chapter 5**

# The Health
# Benefits of Nukazuke Pickles

Fermenting vegetables in a nukazuke pickling bed boosts both their nutritional value as well as their umami. This chapter takes a look at how nukazuke pickles make us healthier, as well as at some of the other fermented foods that have long been enjoyed in Japan and around the world.

# A Probiotic Superfood

### 1. Nukazuke Pickles Improve The Intestinal Environment

The lactic acid bacteria (lactobacilli) living in the nukazuke pickling bed are, as a rule, associated with plants.

Some types of lactobacilli are associated with plants, while others are associated with animals. The latter multiply mainly by feeding on the lactose contained in milk from animals, creating yogurt and cheese. Many of these lactobacilli cannot tolerate environments with a high salt concentration or strong acidity, such as a nukazuke pickling bed.

By contrast, lactobacilli associated with plants feed on the glucose in vegetables. Because they have evolved to endure harsh natural environments, many of them are relatively resistant to the salt content of the pickling bed as well as to stomach acid. As a result, large numbers of these bacteria reach the intestines alive.

Nukazuke contains an abundance of plant-associated lactobacilli (for example, *Lactobacillus plantarum*). Luckily for us, once they reach the intestines, they improve the intestinal environment. Live lactobacilli produce lactic acid in the intestines, making them mildly acidic. Since bad bacteria multiply easily when the pH of the intestines is too high, it is important to maintain a mildly acidic state in order to increase the number of good bacteria.*

Plant-associated lactobacilli also play a role in relieving constipation. Lactic acid stimulates the intestines, promoting peristalsis and facilitating digestive activity. Pickling vegetables that are high in dietary fiber compounds these benefits.

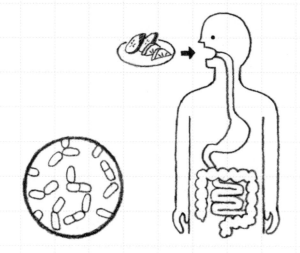

**Plant-Associated Lactobacilli**

Lactobacilli associated with plants are not destroyed by stomach acid, so they reach the intestines alive. There they help create an environment hospitable to good bacteria.

Since lactobacilli tend not to linger in the intestines, the key to sustaining their benefits is to eat nukazuke pickles every day, sending new lactobacilli into your digestive system.

---

*Good bacteria, such as lactobacilli and yeast, have a beneficial effect on humans, while bad bacteria produce harmful substances that cause aging and lifestyle-related diseases. The number of bacteria in a person's intestines is said to exceed 100 trillion, with the good, bad, and in-between always competing against one another.

### 2. The thiamin in nukazuke relieves fatigue, improves appetite, and promotes digestion

Nukazuke pickles are rich in thiamin. Thiamin is a component of the bran layer of brown rice that is removed during milling and which, together with rice germ, makes up the nuka used to ferment nukazuke pickles. The pickling bed therefore contains high levels of thiamin, which is absorbed by the vegetables in the bed through osmosis.

Thiamin helps the body metabolize carbohydrates and prevents the generation of fatigue-inducing substances. It also breaks down sugar and converts it into energy, and promotes gastrointestinal activity, increasing the appetite and improving digestion.

Like vitamin C, thiamin is water soluble and can only be assimilated by the body in limited quantities at one time. It is also difficult to consume as a regular part of the diet because it is destroyed by heat. Incorporating nukazuke into your daily diet is an easy way to make sure you're getting a steady supply of this important vitamin.

### 3. Vitamin C improves skin health and immunity

Vitamin C is a highly beneficial antioxidant that helps build collagen and suppress harmful reactive oxygen species. Unfortunately, it is water-soluble and heat sensitive, meaning raw foods are the best source. Salads take time to prepare and contain a surprisingly small amount of vitamin C per serving. Nukazuke is an easier way to incorporate a large amount of vitamin C into your diet.

### 4. Enzymes prevent aging

Enzymes are essential for living organisms and are involved in all our vital functions, including respiration, digestion, and nutrient absorption. Our bodies can only produce a limited amount of enzymes on their own, and irregular, unhealthy lifestyles cause them to be depleted rapidly. The enzymes we lack are replenished when we eat fresh food. These are called dietary enzymes. Nukazuke is an ideal way to take in dietary enzymes that are heat sensitive and therefore hard to get from other parts of your diet.

Cucumbers are just one example of a vegetable that becomes more nutritious, with a higher content of vitamins such as thiamin, when fermented in a nukazuke pickling bed.

# A Bounty of Fermented Foods

Fermented foods are prepared around the world, and the Japanese in particular have a long history of skillfully incorporating them into daily life. According to Dr. Shigeo Miyao, who assisted with the writing of this chapter, nukazuke pickles were first made as early as the end of the Kamakura period (1185–1333). Let's takes a look at some of the fermented foods that originated in Japan as well as others that have been enthusiastically adopted from overseas.

### The Origins of Fermented Foods

In Japan, people often say that fermented foods are the best of all medicines, and that if you eat them you'll never need a doctor. As those sayings suggest, our ancestors used their experience and wisdom to develop a variety of fermented foods that helped them stay healthy.

The unique climate of the Japanese archipelago is one factor that enabled its inhabitants to develop outstanding techniques for producing fermented foods. The microorganisms necessary for fermentation thrive in Japan's hot and humid climate, surrounded by the sea on all side. These microorganisms gave rise to unique fermented foods made from rice, beans, and other long-familiar ingredients. Miso, soy sauce and sake are just a few of the Japanese fermented foods that are now attracting worldwide attention for their flavor and nutrition.

Another reason fermented foods took root in Japan is that they keep very well. At a time when many of today's food preservation technologies were not available, fermentation was a useful method of preserving food for long periods because microorganisms suppress the growth of harmful bacteria.

Each region of Japan developed its own varieties of miso and other fermented foods. The map on the facing page shows a sampling of these local specialties.

# Traditional Fermented Foods of Japan

A wide range of unique fermented foods make the most of the ingredients available in each region of Japan. Many of them are still eaten today.

## Shottsuru
The main ingredient in this fish sauce is sailfin sandfish, a fish commonly caught off Akita Prefecture. It has been made since the Edo period (1603–1867).

## Mefun
Made by salting the kidneys of male salmon, *mefun* contains vitamin B12 and is said to cure anemia.

## Heshiko
Heshiko is another name for fish nukazuke. It is made along the Japan Sea coast from mackerel, sardines, squid, pufferfish and other fish.

## Kaburazushi
A traditional fermented sushi from Ishikawa Prefecture. Yellowtail is sandwiched between salted turnips and fermented in a nukazuke pickling bed for about a month.

## Iburigakko
Daikon radishes are dried and smoked over the hearth before fermenting in a nukazuke pickling bed. Savory and smoky.

## Sugukizuke
A very sour Kyoto pickle made by pickling a type of turnip called *suguki* in salt.

## Shinshu Miso
A salty miso from the Japan Alps, where miso-making has flourished since the Kamakura period. Shinshu miso is now enjoyed throughout Japan.

## Goishicha
In this drink from Kochi Prefecture, tea leaves are steamed and fermented using lactobacilli and a type of mold.

## Bettarazuke
This sweet pickle from the greater Tokyo area is made by salting daikon radish and then pickling it with rice, koji and sugar.

## Mugi Miso
This light, sweet barley miso is made by fermenting soybeans with barley malt. It is made throughout western Honshu and Kyushu.

## Funazushi
To make this pungent fermented sushi, carp from Lake Biwa are cured in salt and then fermented in rice and salt.

## Kusaya
For this specialty of the Izu Islands, fish is soaked in saltwater and then dried in the sun. It has a powerful, distinct odor.

## Tofu-yo
Okinawan "island tofu" is fermented with koji, red yeast rice, and Okinawan rice wine. It has a creamy texture and a rich flavor.

## Hatcho Miso
A strong, red-brown miso from Aichi Prefecture made entirely from soybeans. Despite its strong taste, it is relatively low in salt.

# Familiar Fermented Foods

### Miso

Introduced from China, miso was being eaten in Japan by the Heian period (794–1185). Koji mold is encouraged to grow on steamed rice or wheat, which is then mixed with steamed soybeans, salt, and other ingredients and allowed to ferment and mature into miso. Rich in essential amino acids and vitamins, miso is said to "keep the doctor away."

### Vinegar

Vinegar has long been made around the world from rice, wheat, apples, grapes, and other foods that contain sugars. These ingredients are first fermented to make alcohol, and then the alcohol is fermented by acetic acid bacteria to make vinegar. The acidity and aroma of vinegar stimulate the appetite, and its antiseptic effects help preserve food.

### Soy Sauce

At the end of the 16th century, the first stores specializing in soy sauce opened around Osaka and Kyoto, later expanding to Edo (now Tokyo). Soy sauce contains gamma-aminobutyric acid, a type of amino acid with tranquilizing effects. It is made by fermenting a mash made from soybeans, wheat, and other ingredients with koji mold, yeast and lactobacilli.

### Shio Koji

Although shio koji (lit. "salt koji") is currently enjoying a popularity boom, it has been used as a seasoning since ancient times. It is made by adding salt and water to rice inoculated with koji mold. When foods like meat and fish are pickled in the resulting slurry, proteins break down and flavor components such as amino acids are produced. Rich in B vitamins, shio koji is nicknamed the "universal seasoning" in Japan.

### Mirin

Authentic mirin is made by aging steamed glutinous rice with koji and alcohol, which breaks down the proteins and starches in the rice and produces amino acids and other substances that create flavor. It was enjoyed as a beverage until the Edo period (1603–1867), after which it came to be used for cooking as well.

### Fermentation vs. ripening

Fermentation is the result of action by microorganisms, while ripening is a metabolic process caused mainly by enzymes that occur naturally in fruits and other foods.

### Katsuobushi

Popular since the Edo period, katsuobushi flakes are used to make stock and season many dishes. To make it, bonito is boiled, then smoked and dried. It is then inoculated with mold and fermented, which removes more of its moisture and lengthens its shelf life.

### Amazake

When koji mold is added to cooked rice, the starch in the rice breaks down to glucose, giving this beverage a unique aroma and sweetness. Although the word "amazake" contains the character for sake, it is not true sake and contains almost no alcohol. It does contain many vitamins and nutrients, however, and is viewed as a natural energy drink in Japan.

### Wine

Yeast breaks down the sugar in grapes to produce alcohol. The wine is then aged in barrels for a long period to develop flavor. Polyphenols, known for their antioxidant effects and prevention of lifestyle-related diseases, are more abundant in red wine, which is fermented without removing the grape skins and seeds.

## Beer

Barley malt is first saccharified to make wort, which is then fermented by adding beer yeast. Beer is believed to have been used as a nutritional supplement in Europe during the Middle Ages. It also has a diuretic effect due to the action of alcohol and potassium.

## Shochu

Shochu is a distilled liquor; unlike beer or sake, it does not contain sugar. The main ingredient, which can range from rice and barley to brown sugar and sweet potatoes, is brewed with koji mold and yeast. The resulting fermented mash is then distilled to remove the sugars and increase alcohol content. Okinawan awamori is another type of distilled liquor.

## Sake

Steamed rice is saccharified by mixing with koji mold and water. Yeast is then added to ferment the starter mash, which promotes alcohol production. The finished product is pressed. Often called "the best of all medicines," sake contains many amino acids that boost immunity, relieve fatigue, and beautify the skin.

## Makgeolli

Makgeolli has been made on the Korean peninsula since ancient times. Koji mold and yeast act on rice, the main ingredient, saccharifying it and producing alcohol. At the same time, lactic acid fermentation also occurs, adding sourness. Since makgeolli contains a large amount of plant-associated lactobacilli, that reach the intestines alive, it is thought to aid digestion.

## Pu'er Tea

This traditional Chinese tea is made by heating and drying tea leaves, then fermenting with molds. Black tea, green tea, and oolong tea are all made from the leaves of the same plant, differing only in their degree of oxidation. The oxidation of these teas is caused by enzymes in the tea leaves themselves, in contrast to the fermentation of pu'er tea caused by microorganisms.

## Shiokara

Shiokara is a salted fermented fish often enjoyed as an appetizer with sake. Many kinds of seafood are used, including squid, octopus, sea urchin, and skipjack tuna. All are prepared by salting and aging the flesh and entrails. The fermentation process utilizes the digestive enzymes of microorganisms and internal organs, which produce the umami and unique smell of shiokara.

## Natto

*Bacillus natto* is a type of bacterium that is abundant in rice straw and other dry plant materials. In the past, natto was made by fermenting boiled soybeans in a bundle of straw, which was boiled first to kill off all but the *bacillus natto*. Natto contains many nutrients, such as riboflavin and vitamin K2.

## Doubanjiang

Fava beans are the main ingredient in this spicy Chinese bean paste, which adds flavor to a variety of dishes such as stir-fries and soups. It is made by slowly fermenting raw or steamed favas with koji, salt, and chili peppers. It was originally made without chili peppers.

## Kimchi

Kimchi is made from napa cabbage, daikon radishes, cucumbers, and other ingredients, to which salt, chili peppers and other flavorings are added. It is fermented mainly by plant-associated lactobacilli. The lactic acid produced by these bacteria and the dietary fiber in the vegetables are said to regulate digestion.

## Menma

Menma are fermented dried bamboo shoots, a staple for topping ramen noodles. They are widely produced in China and Taiwan and have long been eaten in Okinawa as well. Menma are made by boiling the shoots of a species called sweet bamboo and fermenting them with lactobacilli for more than a month. They are high in dietary fiber.

## Tempeh

Tempeh is a traditional fermented food from Indonesia, where it is still frequently eaten. It is made by fermenting boiled soybeans with a mold starter, and contains protein, vitamins, and essential amino acids. Tempeh has a mild flavor and can be eaten deep-fried, boiled, or stir fried.

## Cured ham

Pork legs are salted, dried, and cured to make ham. They can be either smoked or not; the non-smoked type is called prosciutto. In Europe some hams are cured for several years, which enhances the flavor.

## Yogurt

Yogurt is created by lactobacilli that feed on lactose, which is mainly found in animal milk.

The bacteria is added to milk and allowed to ferment. Many lactobacilli associated with animal products are killed by stomach acid, but some survive to regulate the intestines and enhance the immune system.

## Nata de coco

Nata de coco is a fermented food that originated in the Philippines in the mid twentieth century. A type of acetic acid bacteria is added to coconut water, which ferments and solidifies. It is high in dietary fiber.

## Bread

Bread has been made in Europe since prehistoric times. Yeast or other starters are added to dough and fermented. The dough rises because of the yeast's ability to produce carbon dioxide gas. Japan's first sweet bread, anpan, used sake starter made with rice, koji and water.

## Cheese

The milk used to make cheese comes from cows, goats, sheep and other animals. The milk is coagulated by lactobacilli and coagulant enzymes, then ripened by mold and bacteria. Depending on the type of microorganism used, many different cheeses can be made, such as Camembert, Swiss and Gorgonzola. Cheese is rich in calcium and protein.

# Conclusion

I started making nukazuke pickles 15 or 16 years ago. I had a plot in a community garden where I was growing vegetables, but soon I had too many to eat on my own. I wondered what to do with the bounty. What came to mind was nukazuke pickling, which my grandmother had long done.

My grandmother's pickling bed was in a barrel so large it could easily fit a small child inside. As a young girl, I used to mix the pickling bed with my grandmother, excitedly wondering what would be in it that day.

I decided to start my own pickling bed using my memories of my grandmother's techniques as a guide, but at first everything went wrong. There was mold and terrible smells. But I didn't give up, and repeated trial and error eventually led to solutions for most of my pickling problems. These days I enjoy tasty nukazuke pickles every day.

Nukazuke pickles served with freshly cooked rice and miso soup are the secret to my family's health and happiness. My wish is that all readers of this book may enjoy both the delicious flavors of nukazuke pickles and the wonderful health benefits of microorganisms.

## "Books to Span the East and West"

**Tuttle Publishing** was founded in 1832 in the small New England town of Rutland, Vermont [USA]. Our core values remain as strong today as they were then—to publish best-in-class books which bring people together one page at a time. In 1948, we established a publishing outpost in Japan—and Tuttle is now a leader in publishing English-language books about the arts, languages and cultures of Asia. The world has become a much smaller place today and Asia's economic and cultural influence has grown. Yet the need for meaningful dialogue and information about this diverse region has never been greater. Over the past seven decades, Tuttle has published thousands of books on subjects ranging from martial arts and paper crafts to language learning and literature—and our talented authors, illustrators, designers and photographers have won many prestigious awards. We welcome you to explore the wealth of information available on Asia at **www.tuttlepublishing.com**.

Published by Tuttle Publishing, an imprint of
Periplus Editions (HK) Ltd.

www.tuttlepublishing.com

ISBN 978-4-8053-1790-7

HAJIMERU, TSUZUKERU. NUKAZUKE NO KIHON
Copyright © 2016 Nami Yamada
Copyright © 2016 GRAPHIC-SHA PUBLISHING CO., LTD.
This book was first designed and published in Japan in 2016 by
Graphic-sha Publishing Co., Ltd.

The English edition was published in 2024 by Tuttle Publishing
English translation rights arranged with
GRAPHIC-SHA PUBLISHING CO., LTD. through
Japan UNI Agency, Inc., Tokyo

English translation © 2024 Periplus Editions (HK) Ltd.
Translated from the Japanese by Makiko Itoh

*Original Japanese edition creative staff*
**Book design** Yuichi Urushihara (tento)
**Photos** Yukie Yasuhiko
**Illustrations** Yukari Kawanaka
**Editing** Kumi Ohba (Graphic-sha Publishing Co., Ltd.)
**Foreign edition production and management** Takako Motoki
   (Graphic-sha Publishing Co., Ltd.)

Distributed by:

**North America, Latin America
& Europe**
Tuttle Publishing
364 Innovation Drive
North Clarendon
VT 05759–9436 U.S.A.
Tel: (802) 773-8930
info@tuttlepublishing.com
www.tuttlepublishing.com

**Japan**
Tuttle Publishing
Yaekari Building 3rd Floor
5-4-12 Osaki Shinagawa-ku
Tokyo 141 0032
Tel: (81) 3 5437-0171
Fax: (81) 3 5437-0755
sales@tuttle.co.jp
www.tuttle.co.jp

**Asia Pacific**
Berkeley Books Pte. Ltd.
3 Kallang Sector, #04-01
Singapore 349278
Tel: (65) 6741-2178
Fax: (65) 6741-2179
inquiries@periplus.com.sg
www.tuttlepublishing.com

Printed in China   2312EP

27 26 25 24
10 9 8 7 6 5 4 3 2 1